Unequal But Fair.

A Study of Class Barriers in Britain

The IEA Health and Welfare Unit

Choice in Welfare No. 28

Unequal But Fair?

A Study of Class Barriers in Britain

Peter Saunders

IEA Health and Welfare Unit
London, 1996

First published July 1996

The IEA Health and Welfare Unit
2 Lord North St
London SW1P 3LB

© The IEA Health and Welfare Unit 1996

ISBN 0-255 36366-4

Front cover graphics from CorelDraw 6.

Typeset by the IEA Health and Welfare Unit
in New Century Schoolbook 10 on 11 point
Printed in Great Britain by
St Edmundsbury Press Ltd
Blenheim Industrial Park, Newmarket Rd
Bury St Edmunds, Suffolk

Contents

Page

Foreword

If you are able and hard working, can you succeed in Britain? Or do your chances depend on the social class of your parents?

Much of our literature and television drama presents Britain as a class-divided society. Moreover, a couple of generations of social scientists since the Second World War have produced studies claiming that working-class children are born into disadvantage.

Professor Peter Saunders of the University of Sussex tests their claims against the evidence of the National Child Development Study which has followed the lives of a group of children since their birth in 1958. Now in their late thirties, we can study how they have fared during their school years and their early working lives.

The evidence reveals that social class has not been a disadvantage to able and hard-working children. Professor Saunders systematically refutes claims of the older generation of sociologists who typically claim that Britain suffers from a rigid class system, which has suppressed talent and denied opportunity. Britain is not an equal society, he concludes, but it offers a fair chance to anyone with the ability and the will to succeed.

Many sociologists continue to uphold the myth of a class-divided society, despite evidence to the contrary. It remains to be seen whether Britain's sociologists will respond to Professor Saunders' authoritative challenge in a spirit of scholarship, or by means of the 'ritual denunciation' that has become commonplace on some of our campuses.

David G. Green

The Author

Peter Saunders is Professor of Sociology at the University of Sussex where he has worked for the last twenty years, during which time he has also held visiting positions at universities in Australia, New Zealand, Germany and the United States. Born in 1950 and brought up in Croydon, he studied sociology as an undergraduate at the University of Kent and completed a PhD at the University of London in 1975. He has written or co-authored eight academic books which include a brief guide to sociological work on class and inequality, *Social Class and Stratification*, 1990; a study of home ownership in Britain, *A Nation of Home Owners*, 1990; and an analysis of the social effects of privatisation in the 1980s, *Privatization and Popular Capitalism*, 1994. His most recent book, published last year, was *Capitalism: A Social Audit*. He lives in Brighton and has two children: Michael, who is training to be a mental nurse, and Claire, who works for a software marketing company.

Acknowledgements

Initial research for this book was carried out while on a study leave which was supported by a grant from the Economic and Social Research Council. The research subsequently benefited enormously from growing collaboration with Dr. Rod Bond, a colleague at Sussex who early on developed a strong interest in the study, who has offered a lot of help with various problems along the way, and who has ended up working jointly with me on the project. The data analysis on which chapter 8 is based is mainly the product of his work, and I wish to express my gratitude to him for all that he has done. I also wish to thank Bob Blackburn, Alan Buckingham, G. de Barra, Geoff Evans, David Hitchin, Gordon Marshall, Geoff Payne, Ken Prandy, Peter Shepherd and two anonymous referees for their comments, help or guidance, and I am grateful to David Green for encouraging me to produce this book in the first place.

What We All Think We Know About The British Class System

MY FATHER was born into a working-class family in Croydon, the son of a painter and decorator employed by the London County Council. When he left his elementary school at the age of fourteen, just before the war, he asked various of his teachers to sign his autograph book. One of them signed the book and wrote: "Aim high, for though you may not reach the sky, you will most certainly reach the mountain-tops." My father went off to work in a local factory, joined the RAF at the age of 17, and after the war trained to become a teacher. He recently retired after forty successful years in the teaching profession.

There is nothing unusual or remarkable about my father's career history. Millions of men and women have worked their way up to responsible positions in society having started life in relatively humble surroundings. Margaret Thatcher was, after all, the daughter of a Grantham grocer, and John Major's father worked in a circus. Throughout business, the professions and the public services we find examples of individuals who have made good as a result of their own abilities and their own efforts, people who 'aimed high' and reached or even surpassed the mountain-tops.

In one of his first speeches after assuming the premiership, John Major made clear his commitment to the principle that *any* individual should be able to achieve success in life provided only that they have the necessary talent and that they are prepared to work hard in pursuit of their objective. What this speech shared in common with the inscription in my father's autograph book was a belief in the principle of *meritocracy*.

The word was coined in 1958 by Michael Young in his widely-read and influential book *The Rise of the Meritocracy 1870-2033*. In this book, Young detected a growing emphasis on social recruitment based, not on social origins, but on individual talent and motivation, and he anticipated a time when the higher occupational positions in British society would all be filled by the most able and hard-working individuals. Young went on to forecast that such a society would run into severe problems as a result of the disaffection of the less talented and less committed majority at the base of the social pyramid, and this is an issue which we shall need to address in the final chapter of this book. For the moment, however, we need only note Young's definition of 'merit' as consisting of "intelligence and effort together".[1]

Today, in Britain, there appears to be widespread support for this principle of meritocratic selection. When he assumed the leadership of the

Labour Party, for example, Mr. Blair made clear that, like Mr. Major, he too was committed to the idea that ability and hard work should determine an individual's place in society. New Labour, it seems, has jettisoned the belief in equalising outcomes irrespective of differences of merit between individuals. Provided they compete on a level playing field, Mr. Blair seems quite content to allow individuals to rise or fall on the basis of their own efforts.

But is there a level playing field? Evidently, neither Mr. Major nor Mr. Blair believe that there is, for both of them have made clear their desire to turn Britain into a meritocratic society. This implies that our society currently falls a long way short of this ideal and that social origins still count for too much in influencing social destinations.

In arguing this way, both party leaders are expressing a view which appears to be widely held within the British public as a whole. Something approaching two-thirds of the public believe that class background affects people's opportunities 'quite a lot' or 'a great deal', and only one in twenty believe that it has no effect.[2] Asked to explain why some people live in relative need, nearly twice as many people put it down to bad luck or 'social injustice' than to individual characteristics such as laziness or lack of motivation.[3] Like John Major and Tony Blair, many British people evidently believe that individual merit should be the decisive factor in determining where we all end up in life, but that, in reality, this ideal is constantly subverted by the continuing influence which social background has on individual achievement.

Some years ago, Professor Peter Bauer attacked what he termed a 'British obsession' with class. Britain, he argued, sees itself, and is seen by others, as *peculiarly* divided by class when in reality it is a remarkably open society. There is, he said, a strong and pervasive myth that, in Britain, class divisions are sharper and more enduring than in other western industrialised countries, and it is widely accepted that social movement between classes is rare and difficult to achieve. Bauer cited anecdotal and sociological evidence to suggest otherwise.[4]

In this book, I shall attempt to show that the folk wisdom in Britain has basically got it wrong, and that Professor Bauer was basically right. The evidence I shall review strongly suggests that, while Britain is not a perfect meritocracy, it is a lot more meritocratic than many of us seem to believe. If I am correct in this argument, however, then we need to ask why the 'British obsession' remains so entrenched.

Part of the explanation has to do with our history. In comparison with most of the countries of continental Europe, Britain has a unique history of institutional continuity. The nation has successfully avoided colonisation or conquest ever since the Norman invasion nearly one thousand years ago, and its internal upheavals have been few and, by European standards, relatively modest. Britain is an old society and many of its old institutions have survived in tact. We still have a remarkably traditional monarchy and an Upper House which seems to many modern observers archaic and out of place in a democratic age. We still have an aristocracy with its castles and its grouse moors, and a titled stratum which desports itself regularly in public, eating strawberries at Wimbledon, drinking champagne at Henley, and displaying its finery in the Royal Enclosure at Ascot. Nobody looking at Britain could be left in any doubt that this is a country where inherited privilege still counts for something in the traditional status pecking order.

All too easily, however, we go on to assume that the whole society is like this, that the persistence of social closure at the very top must be reproduced all the way down the class system, and that the relics of a pre-industrial and pre-capitalist social order must still be smothering the whole of modern life. The symbolism of monarchy and aristocracy blinds us to the reality of an open and achievement-oriented society jostling beyond the confines of the Royal Enclosure at Ascot.

Part of the reason for this has to do with our *intelligentsia*. Many of Britain's finest twentieth century novelists, playwrights and television producers have been working-class boys (and occasionally girls) who have 'made good'. So too have many of Britain's leading sociologists. Despite their own history of upward mobility, however, these artists and academics have often developed bitter critiques of what they see as a self-perpetuating 'establishment' which blocks the rise and blights the lives of millions of people just like them who were not 'lucky' enough to escape their lowly origins.

From *The Ragged Trousered Philanthropists* to *The Remains of the Day*, from *Cathy Come Home* to *Boys from the Black Stuff*, British novels, films, plays and (most crucially) television programmes have frequently presented an image of Britain as a class-divided society in which sturdy and honest working-class folk never manage to get off the floor because pampered aristocrats or mean-hearted capitalists are trampling all over them. A principal medium for this message has been comedy, for most British comedy works on pathos (which is why the Americans have so much trouble relating to it), and the key source of pathos is the plight of the working-class (which is why middle-class sit-coms are so rarely successful). As I was growing up, I learned about the tragic fatalism of the working-class from Harry H. Corbett's doomed attempts to escape it in *Steptoe and Son*, and from Rodney Bewes in *The Likely Lads* I learned that you never really escape your working-class origins anyway. I learned about the callous stupidity of the upper class from *Monty Python*'s Upper Class Twit of the Year Show, and Ronnie Corbett, Ronnie Barker and John Cleese taught me all I needed to know about the British class system in their celebrated sketch for *That Was The Week That Was*.

Now it could be objected at this point that dominant images in the popular culture do not get created out of thin air. The reason why these images resonate so strongly within the popular consciousness must surely have something to do with people's everyday experiences in contemporary

Britain, for why else should we accept them as an accurate portrayal of the society in which we live?

One reason why we accept them may be that it suits many of us to believe that we live in a closed and rigid class system. For those of us who fail to achieve success in life, there is the off-the-peg excuse that we never had a chance, that we were bright enough and motivated enough to have done much better but that we were thwarted in our endeavours by a socially unjust system. For those of us who do succeed, by contrast, there is the inner glow, rarely expressed in public, which comes from the knowledge that we made it despite enormous odds, and that we must therefore have had some really quite extraordinary qualities. In polite company, of course, successful, upwardly-mobile individuals generally prefer to shrug their shoulders and put their success down to sheer luck or circumstance, for it is seen as ill-mannered and vulgar to lay claim to special talents marking one out from the mass of one's fellow citizens. Nevertheless, it is noticeable how frequently successful individuals make reference to their (real or imagined) working-class origins, and as Mr. Blair has found, there is little *kudos* to be won by acknowledging a 'privileged' start in life such as wealthy parents or a private education.

We are, therefore, predisposed to believe the myth of social class closure. A further factor which explains it, however, is the great weight of sociological evidence and argument which has for a long time seemed to demonstrate that class divisions in Britain really are rigid and relatively impermeable.

Without unduly exaggerating the social and political influence achieved by the social sciences in Britain, it is surely significant that sociologists have for so long maintained with a remarkable degree of unanimity that the popular myth corresponds closely with the sociological reality. Literally millions of people in Britain have been exposed directly to sociology, and millions more have been indirectly influenced by its arguments and findings. Sociology is a popular 'A'-level subject and sociology courses figure prominently, not only in our universities, but also in vocational training for a range of professions including the police, nursing, social work, teaching and management. Many of the post-war social reforms in Britain—the abolition of educational selection at 11, the adoption and subsequent abandonment of high-rise housing, the reforms of penal policy, and the shift from institutional care of mental patients towards 'care in the community'—have been directly or indirectly influenced by sociological research findings, and one reason why sociology has a reputation for telling us what we already know is precisely that many of its core assumptions and findings have permeated rapidly into the stock of common knowledge.

Here, then, is a key reason why the 'British obsession' remains so pervasive and enduring. It is, quite simply, because the myth of class rigidity has been reinforced for so long by British sociologists. Successive generations of young people have been taught that British society remains relatively closed and that the system is 'unjust', and these same arguments and evidence have then been reproduced and perpetuated in popular form by journalists, politicians and media commentators to a point where it now seems fantastic to assume that it might be otherwise. In Britain, we 'know' that we live in a rigid and unfair society. Even Mr. Major, the circus performer's son from Brixton, 'knows' this, for why else should he have expressed his desire to turn Britain into a meritocracy, rather than telling us that, to a large extent, it already is one?

How Long Are The Snakes,
How Tall Are The Ladders?

I N THIS book I seek to demonstrate, against the popular myth and the received sociological wisdom, that occupational selection and recruitment in Britain is much more meritocratic than most of us realise or care to believe. I must, however, enter two notes of caution at the outset.

First, my concern is with the occupational system, not with traditional élite positions. As I noted in chapter 1, there is still a strong element of inherited privilege associated with certain sections of the British upper class. There is no open competition for the position as the next King, nor do I or others like me stand much chance of accumulating the sort of land and assets bequeathed to the Duke of Westminster. I do not, therefore, claim that *all* positions in British society are filled through open competition on the basis of individual ability and effort, for my focus is on the 99 per cent of jobs below the élite stratum rather than on the 1 per cent which constitute it.

Having said that, it is also necessary to add that, even among the élite, meritocratic recruitment is by no means as rare as is often assumed. Citing various studies of élite recruitment conducted during the 1970s, for example, Anthony Heath shows that 11 per cent of top civil servants, 19 per cent of Church of England bishops, 27 per cent of ambassadors, 28 per cent of High Court judges, and 45 per cent of bank directors had themselves been born to parents occupying élite positions.[1] As Heath points out, even at these rarified heights, recruitment from outside the élite clearly predominates over élite self-recruitment. Similarly, it is clear that many of the richest individuals in Britain have accumulated their wealth through their own efforts rather than through accident of birth. The latest of the annual *Sunday Times* reviews of the richest five hundred people in the country reveals many more 'self-made' men and women than inheritors—among them, household names such as Richard Branson, Alan Sugar, Anita Roddick and Paul McCartney.[2] Even the landed aristocracy is permeable to some extent, for as Peter Bauer points out, this stratum has for eight hundred years been penetrated by those born into lower ranks, either by dint of marriage or through economic success in business.

The second point I wish to emphasise is that, even outside the élite, I do not claim that Britain is a *perfect* meritocracy. The various advantages and disadvantages associated with different social class origins do play some part in influencing people's occupational chances—sociologists over the last fifty years have not been completely wrong or deluded. The point, however, is that Britain is much more meritocratic than is generally believed. Class origins are not very important, nor are the supposed advantages (such as private schooling) enjoyed by children born to more affluent or better-placed parents particularly significant in shaping outcomes. To the extent that it is possible to predict somebody's occupational destiny, it is their ability and their motivation that matters much more than the social class into which they were born. In modern Britain, if you are bright and committed, you are likely to succeed in the occupational system irrespective of where you start out from, and although things are not perfect and the playing field is not completely level, this means that our society is nevertheless remarkably open, and that we are much closer to achieving a meritocracy than pundits and public alike seem to suppose.

For most of the last fifty years, the British sociological community has denied this. No less an esteemed figure than Professor Tawney once dismissed precisely such a claim as "obviously a jest",[3] and down the years, sociologists have argued that meritocracy is no more than an elaborate illusion, an ideological confidence trick designed to win legitimacy for a socially unjust system of class privilege by convincing the losers that the competition has been fair. Certainly, until the late seventies, eminent British sociologists, all of them on the political Left, had taken as given the 'fact' that occupational competition is biased and that the dice are heavily loaded against those from the lower social classes. The consensus among the great and the good of British sociology was unshakeable:

> The social class system ... operates, largely, through the inheritance of property, to ensure that each individual maintains a certain social position, determined by his birth and irrespective of his particular abilities ... Most social mobility takes place between social levels which are close together ... The vast majority of people still remain in their class of origin ... In Britain, all manner of ancient institutions and modes of behaviour—the aristocracy, the public schools, Oxbridge, differences of speech and accent, the relationships of the 'old boy' network—frustrate mobility.[4]
>
> *Professor Tom Bottomore, 1965*

> Those who fear a 'meritocratic' society in which everyone, starting more or less equally, would be judged on 'merit' alone, need not therefore be unduly alarmed: the race is still rigged—against the working-class competitors ... the upper and middle-class ... is still largely self-recruiting and therefore to a marked degree socially cohesive.[5]
>
> *Professor Ralph Miliband, 1969*

> The chances that those born into different social classes will stay in those classes are still very high. Though there is a good deal of mobility, most of it is, in fact, very short range mobility. The myths of 'long distance' mobility—from 'log cabin to President'—are, overwhelmingly, myths as far as the life chances of the mass of the population are concerned ... it is far too simplistic to describe modern society as predominantly 'achievement-oriented'.[6]
>
> *Professor Peter Worsley, 1970*

Virtually all movement, whether upward or downward, inter- or intra-genera-
tional, across the non-manual/manual division is 'short-range' ... There has not
been much change in rates of mobility between manual and non-manual labour
over the period since World War I.[7]

Professor Anthony Giddens, 1973

People are a good deal more likely to stay at roughly the same level as their
fathers than they would be if there were 'perfect mobility' ... Those born into the
top strata have enormous advantages in respect of their job prospects—as in
respect of so much else—over all others; not least in this country. Long distance
movement especially—from bottom to top, as well as from top to bottom—is
uncommon. Most individual mobility is far more modest; and much of it stays on
one side or the other of the conventional dividing line between white- and blue-
collar work ... Movement up and down the ladder is inhibited by sharp inequalities of opportunity.[8]

Professor John Westergaard with Henrietta Resler, 1975

Hence the authoritative voice of the sociological orthodoxy down the
years. But whence the source of this unanimity of belief and assertion? The
answer lies in a piece of research undertaken by Professor David Glass and
some of his colleagues working at the London School of Economics in the
late 1940s.[9] The authors claimed from their study of ten thousand men
that social mobility across anything more than a very short range of
occupational statuses was uncommon in Britain at that time. Their results
referred, of course, to a sample of men most of whom had moved into jobs
long before the Second World War and whose fathers had often started
work long before the First World War, and Glass recognised that the
pattern could change dramatically as a result of reforms such as the 1944
Education Act. Later generations of sociologists ignored all this, however,
and Glass's findings were reproduced uncritically for the next thirty years
as an accurate representation of what was happening in the present. As
late as the mid-1970s, sociology students were still being taught that
Britain was a relatively closed society in which the upper and middle-
classes were generally able to secure their position for the next generation
and where talented children born into the working-class had little realistic
prospect of significant upward movement, even into relatively low-status
white collar jobs.

It is a sad reflection on the rigour, vitality and integrity of much
mainstream post-war British sociology that the Glass findings were so
readily endorsed by so many leading sociologists for so long. The evidence
was hopelessly dated (more than two-thirds of the fathers in the study had
first entered the labour market when Queen Victoria was still on the
British throne), yet these findings were accepted as a valid guide to British
social structure well into the 1970s, thirty years into the long post-war
economic boom and long after the first wave of post-war social and
educational reforms should have had some sort of impact. Even worse, the
research was seriously flawed. Geoff Payne[10] has meticulously demonstrated that the data are unreliable, for taking account of the twentieth
century expansion in white-collar and contraction in blue-collar jobs, and

of the higher fertility rates in working-class than in middle-class families, the Glass data could only have been valid if the number of white collar jobs had declined by 18 per cent in the course of a generation. In reality, however, the number of such jobs had increased over this period by 17 per cent. The findings, in other words, were quite simply impossible given the occupational changes documented by censuses through the first fifty years of this century.

Payne likens David Glass's standing within social mobility research to that of Charles Darwin in evolutionary theory. A more appropriate parallel might be with the infamous Cyril Burt and his influence upon psychological thinking about intelligence. Like Burt, Glass's work went uncriticised for many years despite clear evidence that the data were fallacious. There is no suggestion that Glass manufactured his data, but Payne does note with some frustration the apparent unwillingness within the discipline of sociology to cast doubt upon Glass's study. This may have had something to do with Glass's standing within British sociology, for in the early 1950s he was a major figure with considerable influence, but it also probably reflects the reluctance of left-wing sociologists to question findings which were consistent with their own prejudices. As Payne points out:

> Almost without exception, sociological writers on social class in Britain have adopted a political stance on the Left. When Glass wrote that there was little upward social mobility, it reinforced everything else that they knew about the class system. There was no incentive, therefore, to challenge his results.[11]

Eventually, however, Glass's conclusions were challenged. In what remains the single most important and most rigorous study of social mobility in Britain, carried out in 1972, Professor John Goldthorpe, together with colleagues at Nuffield College, Oxford, finally demonstrated, much to his own surprise, that the fundamental assumptions of so much post-war British sociology were simply wrong. Based upon a national representative sample of ten thousand men, and utilising his own social class schema designed to distinguish class positions on the basis of authority and personal autonomy at work, on the one hand, and market power (i.e. monetary rewards), on the other, Goldthorpe demonstrated a remarkably high degree of social fluidity, both between generations ('intergenerational mobility') and in the course of a single generation ('intragenerational mobility'). Collapsing his class schema into just three main strata—the *service class* (mainly professional, managerial and high-level administrative positions together with owners of large companies), the *intermediate classes* (routine white-collar grades, supervisory workers and owners of small-scale enterprises employing few if any workers), and the *working-class* (skilled, semi-skilled and unskilled manual employees exercising no supervisory functions)—Goldthorpe found that around half of his sample (49 per cent) ended up in a social class which was different from that into which they had been born.

Flying in the face of sociological orthodoxy, Goldthorpe went on to show that there was substantial movement down as well as up the class system (despite the expansion in the number of high-level positions between the time when the fathers entered the labour force and the time when their sons did), and that long-range movement was common, including movement both ways across the supposed white-collar/blue-collar 'barrier'. While 59 per cent of the sons of service class fathers had retained their class position, 26 per cent of them had fallen into the intermediate classes, and 15 per cent had dropped all the way down to the working-class. Similarly, while 57 per cent of working-class sons had remained in the class to which they had been born, 27 per cent had entered intermediate class positions and 16 per cent had risen into the service class.

Thinking that these results may have been a peculiar product of the long post-war boom, and that the onset of recession from the mid-1970s might have led to subsequent diminution in social mobility rates, Goldthorpe went on in 1983 to conduct further research. Again, his results came as a surprise, for, rather than narrowing, the chances of social movement had if anything expanded still further in the intervening decade! By 1983, more than half (53 per cent) of the sample had changed classes, and the chances of working-class upward movement had markedly improved. By 1983, the proportion of working-class sons entering the service class had risen from 16 per cent to 22 per cent, while the proportion remaining where they had started had fallen from 57 per cent to 47 per cent.

Such evidence on what Goldthorpe termed the 'absolute rates' of social mobility was enough to convince him that the post-war sociological orthodoxy, which had been so uncritically relayed for so long to an unsuspecting public, would have to be overthrown. What he called the 'closure thesis' (which held that top positions are self-recruiting), the 'buffer zone thesis' (which claimed that movement across long distances was severely restricted), and the 'counterbalance thesis' (which suggested that any increase in intergenerational social mobility chances had been countered by a decrease in the opportunities for intragenerational movement), were all finally refuted.

Further studies by other researchers during the 1980s only confirmed Goldthorpe's findings. At the University of Essex, for example, Gordon Marshall and his colleagues found in their national survey that one-third of all men and women in the service class had started life in the manual working-class,[12] and in Scotland, Geoff Payne found that membership of even the most senior levels of the service class was extremely unstable, only a minority managing to retain such positions across more than one generation, and 14 per cent of service class children ending up in manual working-class jobs.[13] Meanwhile, John Goldthorpe has gone on to compare social mobility rates across different countries and has found that downward social mobility (arguably the acid test of an open society in a situation where the number of higher level jobs is expanding while those at the lower levels are contracting) is higher in England and Scotland than in any other of the nations included in the analysis.[14]

Old prejudices, however, die hard. For more than ten years, we have known that our prevailing ideas about social mobility were wrong, but this has not stopped left-wing sociologists from reproducing the old myths. In 1992, for example, Richard Scase published a student text, simply entitled *Class*, in which he authoritatively reasserted the familiar orthodoxy:

> There is a high degree of intergenerational inheritance of managerial and professional jobs on the one hand, and of manual occupations on the other. If there is any intergenerational openness it is among lower grade technical, lesser professional and routine non-manual occupations.[15]

Such a claim is difficult to reconcile with Goldthorpe's evidence showing that, by 1983, 22 per cent of children of working-class origins were found in the service class, and that 38 per cent of children born into the service class were downwardly mobile.

How is it that such claims are still being made in British sociology despite the clear evidence from Goldthorpe's work and from other studies that they are palpably false? Part of the answer is probably that British sociology is still strongly biased towards the Left and that it will take more than the mere weight of empirical evidence to convince some British sociologists that the time has come finally to abandon their cherished but discredited myths. But there is another factor, too, for Goldthorpe's results were not as simple as they seemed. Indeed, having demolished the conventional sociological wisdom in the first part of his book, Goldthorpe went on to reconstruct it, albeit in a more sophisticated form, in the second part, and it may be this which has encouraged other sociologists, like Richard Scase, to reaffirm their faith in the old orthodoxy. The question of how Goldthorpe managed to pull off this conjuring trick in the face of his own empirical findings is one which we shall now go on to consider.

The Dwarf, the Giant and the Hot-Air Balloon

FIRST, let us recap. Dividing the population into three basic social classes, John Goldthorpe found that half of all adult men in Britain are in a different social class than the one to which their fathers belonged at the equivalent age. The British class system is remarkably fluid.

When he focused only on the higher echelons within what he called the 'service class'—i.e. the higher grade professionals, managers, administrators and large proprietors who generally enjoy the highest salaries and exercise the most authority in our society—Goldthorpe found that only a quarter of them had fathers who had occupied equivalent positions. Three-quarters, in other words, had been upwardly mobile into these positions, and 29 per cent of them had risen all the way up from manual working-class origins. Even the most senior positions at the top of the occupational system, therefore, recruit widely among individuals from all class backgrounds. Social mobility is common, even between the extremes of the class system.

Goldthorpe further showed that being born to 'service class' parents is no guarantee of one's own future occupational success. Fewer than six in every ten sons of service class fathers in Goldthorpe's survey themselves went on to occupy service class positions, and more than four in ten were downwardly mobile. Sixteen per cent of those born into the service class ended up sliding all the way down the longest snake into the manual working-class.

There is, therefore, a lot of movement within the British class system—over long distances as well as short, and downwards as well as up. As we have seen, such evidence forced John Goldthorpe to the conclusion that conventional sociological thinking about class and social mobility in Britain was simply wrong.

But this was not the end of the story. The evidence reviewed so far refers to what Goldthorpe calls 'absolute' rates of social mobility, but he went on to suggest that it is also important to investigate 'relative' rates. When he did this, the overall message from his research changed dramatically.

What is at issue in the analysis of relative mobility rates is the changing character of the class system over time. As a result of long-term economic growth, technological development and expansion of state employment during the twentieth century, the number of mundane, manual jobs has been declining, and there has been an enormous expansion in the number of higher grade positions. The British economy has been in transition from reliance on manufacturing to ever-increasing reliance on services, and many of the new service-sector jobs entail higher levels of remuneration, autonomy, responsibility and security than those which they have replaced. Put simply, the occupational system has itself become 'more middle-class'.

Comparing any one generation with the one which preceded it, the chances of attaining a higher level position have therefore been improving. It is in consequence no surprise to find that large numbers of people born to working-class parents end up in higher social classes, for with an expansion of 'room at the top', some degree of upward mobility is inevitable. There are too few children born to 'service class' parents to fill all the new 'service class' positions, so some children from lower social classes must be 'sucked upwards' to plug the shortfall in the number of recruits.

It was for this reason that Goldthorpe moved beyond his analysis of absolute rates of mobility to focus on relative rates as the most appropriate measure of genuine fluidity and openness. For him, the acid test was not whether large numbers of people were upwardly mobile, but was whether working-class children had improved their chances of occupational success *relative to the chances enjoyed by children born into higher social classes*. Everybody today has a better chance of success than their parents did, simply because there are now more positions to fill at the higher levels. The question, however, is whether there has been any change in the relative chances of success enjoyed by children from different social class backgrounds.

Goldthorpe's answer to this was, emphatically, that very little had changed. Working-class children had always been less likely to succeed than middle-class children, and this was just as true today as it had been in the past. The expansion of top positions had been equally advantageous to the children of all social classes so that the gap between them in terms of their relative chances of success was as wide as ever. Goldthorpe concluded that there was "little if any evidence of progress having been made" towards greater openness in the class system, and that "no significant reduction in class inequalities was in fact achieved" during the post-war period, despite the expansion of educational opportunities for working-class children since 1944.[1] A similar conclusion was also drawn by the Essex University team when they investigated relative social mobility rates in their survey. Like Goldthorpe, they claimed on the basis of their results that, "The post-war project of creating in Britain a more open society ... has signally failed to secure its objective".[2]

The evidence for these assertions is provided in the form of what are called 'disparity ratios' and 'odds ratios'. Disparity ratios express the relative likelihood of children from different social class origins arriving at the same social class destination.[3] In Goldthorpe's 1972 survey there was a disparity ratio of nearly 4:1 comparing the chances of service class children and working-class children achieving a service class position. Comparing different birth cohorts within the sample, Goldthorpe was able to demonstrate that this ratio had remained fairly constant over time, although his follow-up 1983 survey did indicate that the disparity had fallen during the previous decade from around 4:1 to around 3:1. The fundamental conclusion arising from all this was that there were persisting inequalities in chances of success for children from different social class origins. If your father was in a professional, managerial or administrative job, then you were three or four times more likely to achieve such a position yourself than if your father was in a manual working-class occupation.

The second measure of relative social mobility used by Goldthorpe involved 'odds ratios'. Odds ratios combine lower class chances of success and higher class chances of failure in the same measure. They are a statistical construct which cannot easily be translated into everyday language, but they are important in Goldthorpe's analysis since they are the basis of the modelling technique which he uses (known as 'loglinear modelling').[4]

Odds ratios are constructed in three stages. First, we have to calculate the chances of a child from the highest social class falling to the lowest class. If, for example, 50 per cent of service class children retain their position while 10 per cent fall all the way down to the working-class, this gives them a 5:1 chance of ending up in the working-class as against remaining in the service class (even though the chance of remaining in the service class is evens). Second, a similar calculation is made regarding the chances of a child from working-class origins rising all the way up to a service class position as compared with the likelihood of remaining in the working-class. If, say, 60 per cent of working-class children end up in working-class jobs while 20 per cent make it to the top, this would give each working-class child a 3:1 chance of getting to the top as against remaining where they started from. Third, these two sets of disparity ratios are then expressed in relation to each other by multiplying the first by the second. In our hypothetical example, this would produce a final odds ratio of 15 (5:1 against service class downward mobility multiplied by 3:1 against working-class upward mobility).

In Goldthorpe's 1972 survey, the odds ratios for different birth cohorts of service class and working-class men ranged between 13 and 19. These figures became even greater when the top of the service class (Goldthorpe's class I, the higher level professional, managerial and administrative jobs together with large proprietors) was compared with the bottom of the working-class (class VII, the semi- and unskilled manual workers). Taking these extreme points of the class system as the basis for comparison, Goldthorpe ended up with odds ratios as high as 36.

It is important not to confuse disparity ratios and odds ratios. Odds ratios do not tell us the relative chances of success or failure of children from different social backgrounds. For this, we should look to the disparity ratios. Odds ratios are extreme measures which combine success and failure chances in a single statistic and which therefore multiply up any apparent class advantages or disadvantages enjoyed by one group relative to another. Suppose, for example, that employers began to adopt 'positive discrimination' or 'affirmative action' policies as part of a deliberate strategy designed to favour working-class applicants for middle-class jobs. The result would certainly be a reduction in the size of disparity ratios, but this would not necessarily be reflected in any significant reduction of odds ratios, for such a reduction would also require that middle-class children become simultaneously less successful at achieving top positions and/or that more of them end up sliding all the way down the class system. A significant narrowing of odds ratios, in other words, requires not only that working-class chances improve, but also that middle-class chances deteriorate—there would need to be 'levelling down' as well as 'levelling up'. Given that the number of top jobs is expanding while positions at the bottom are contracting, it is asking a lot to expect that middle-class downward mobility should rise at the same time as working-class upward mobility is increasing, in which case odds ratios are always likely to remain large.

Odds ratios, then, are useful statistical artifacts, but isolated from the technical context of statistical modelling in which they are meant to be applied, they can be misleading as indicators of the relative openness of a class system. It is unfortunate, then, that in the course of his book, Goldthorpe tended to refer to what he terms 'gross' odds ratios, rather than to the more modest disparity ratios, as evidence of the apparent 'unfairness' of contemporary British society.[5] It is on the disparity ratios of around 3:1 or 4:1, rather than on odds ratios as high as 30:1 or more, that we need to concentrate if we are to judge the degree to which children from different social origins differ in their social mobility chances.

Of course, even the disparity ratios look high. If working-class children are three or four times less likely than middle-class children to get into middle-class jobs, and are three or four times more likely than their middle-class contemporaries to end up in working-class jobs, then isn't this in itself good enough evidence to support the claim that there is no 'level playing field' and that some children are gaining unfair advantages over others by virtue of their social class background? Are not sociologists like John Goldthorpe and the Essex University team justified in asserting that little has really changed over the last fifty years in Britain and that we still live, as we always have done, in a society which is fundamentally unfair and unjust?

There are two good reasons for hesitating before we leap to such a conclusion. The first is that an emphasis on *relative* measures, be they disparity ratios or odds ratios, tends to distract us from what is arguably the more significant evidence regarding *absolute* rates of social mobility. The second is that the emphasis on relative *outcomes* neglects the fundamentally important issue of how and why different individuals are recruited to the positions at which they finally arrive—i.e. the *routes* through which individuals achieve success or failure.

The first point can usefully be illustrated by means of an analogy. Suppose a one-metre dwarf and a three-metre giant together decide that they wish to explore the skies above their heads by hiring a hot air balloon. As they rise above the ground, both clearly benefit from an enhanced view, but the dwarf never gets his or her head to the level enjoyed by the giant. If we insist on measuring their ascent purely in relative terms (i.e. relative to each other), we shall conclude that nothing significant has changed—the 'disparity ratio' is, as it always was, 3:1 in favour of the giant. The fact that both of them are now many times higher than they were before they entered the balloon is dismissed as unimportant or uninteresting, yet it is their joint ascent which is in reality far more crucial in determining the quality of the view which they can each now achieve.

Like the dwarf and the giant, the working-class and the middle-class have shared equally in a marked improvement in their chances of achieving a high position, and it is this which has arguably had the major impact on our lives. Goldthorpe's own survey demonstrates (through an analysis of his respondents' life history notes) that the primary concern for most people is not whether their children's opportunities have improved relative to other people's, but is whether their children have a better chance of succeeding today than they did in the past. As Geoff Payne has argued in respect of Goldthorpe's emphasis on relative measures:

> It is essentially a pessimistic view which leads the reader towards seeing British society as more closed and thereby more *static* than is necessary ... There is considerable fluidity; certainly sufficient fluidity to require of us as sociologists that we come to terms with it. Goldthorpe directs our attention away from it, in part because of the narrow view of his subject, derived from his political position, and in part because he underestimates the significance of the key process in mobility, namely occupational transition ...[6]

The important thing for most of us is precisely the change which relative measures seek to obscure—namely, that there is now much more room at the top so that all classes have a better chance of achieving a well-paid and fulfilling position than their parents or their grandparents enjoyed.

The second problem with this whole tradition of work on relative social mobility rates, and the more serious of my two objections, concerns the failure to analyse why individuals achieve the positions which they do. Ever since the pioneering research of David Glass in the 1940s, social mobility research in Britain has been carried out mainly by left-wing sociologists wedded to a conception of 'social justice' which focuses exclusively on the unequal 'distribution' of end results rather than on the ways in which such unequal outcomes arise in the first place. From this perspective, if we discover inequalities in outcomes, then this alone is sufficient evidence to demonstrate 'unfairness' and 'injustice' in the social system.[7] The fact that middle-class children are more successful on average than working-class children is therefore taken as evidence that the society in which we live is unjustly discriminating in favour of the former and against the latter.

There is, however, another possibility. What if middle-class children are on average brighter than working-class children, or if they work harder on average than their working-class peers? Under meritocratic conditions, we should then expect the children of the middle-classes to fare better in the occupational system, for a meritocracy is precisely a system which allocates positions on the basis of ability and effort.

This possibility is effectively ruled out by sociologists like Goldthorpe and Marshall due to the way they interpret their relative mobility measures. Whether they focus on disparity ratios or odds ratios, the criterion of social justice or fairness which they adopt is the base point of unity, a ratio of 1:1. For them, a fair and open society would be one where all children from whatever social origins have exactly the same statistical chance of ending up in any given occupation at any point in the class system. Goldthorpe and Marshall are not interested in the crucial question of how and why these children arrive at their destinations, only in the end pattern of their distribution across the occupational system. For them, the sons and daughters of doctors should be neither more nor less likely to achieve a middle-class position than the daughters and sons of dockers, for it is assumed that there are no differences of ability or motivation between them. Any ratio in excess of unity—i.e. any evidence that class destinations are not randomly distributed in comparison with class origins—is simply assumed to indicate that the society is treating different groups unfairly.

This type of reasoning entirely ignores the question of whether some children are more talented or more hard-working than others, for, if they are, they should clearly be expected to succeed more readily under conditions of meritocracy. What if the sons and daughters of doctors are, *on average*, more talented or more motivated than the sons and daughters of dockers? If this were the case, evidence on relative social mobility rates would of itself tell us nothing about the fairness of the system, for we would then *expect* children from certain social origins to perform better than those from others. In this case, insisting on a fairness criterion of 1:1 disparity or odds ratios would be absurd.

In his work, John Goldthorpe sees any disparity ratio or odds ratio in excess of 1:1 as indicative of the existence of social barriers which must be blocking working-class children from rising in the social structure while safeguarding middle-class children from falling. He does not bother to investigate what these barriers might be—they are simply assumed to exist from the fact that the disparity and odds ratios are higher than unity. It is this assumption which then enables him to assert that:

> The reality of contemporary British society most strikingly and incontrovertibly deviates from the ideal of genuine openness.[8]

But this conclusion only follows if we neglect to consider the issues of talent and motivation—the very issues which should lie at the heart of any analysis of meritocracy!

We shall see in chapter six that, once we allow for class variations in average levels of ability and motivation, the relative mobility rates which have been reported in the sociological literature appear remarkably consistent with what we should expect to find in a genuinely open and meritocratic society. Far from deviating from the 'ideal of genuine openness', Goldthorpe's own evidence seems to suggest that this ideal may in fact have already been achieved. Before considering this evidence, however, it is necessary to confront a question which most of British sociology has tried to avoid for the last thirty years—the question of whether average levels of ability vary across different social classes.

Intelligence: The Great Taboo

THE United States Constitution famously proclaims that all human beings are 'born equal'. Back in the late eighteenth century, this meant that all human beings should be able to claim equal *rights* under the law. Those who framed the Constitution did not for one moment believe that all human beings were literally born the same: they knew that some are born tall and some short, that some are born strong and some weak, that some are born with many talents while others are born with few. It also has to be said that they did not even believe that all human beings were born with equal rights, for the men who drew up the Constitution did not think of extending this principle to women, to native American Indians, or to black slaves transported from Africa. Nevertheless, their basic sentiment was clear enough. They recognised that people are all different, but they believed that these differences did not in principle justify either governments or courts of law discriminating between them in the way they are treated.[1]

Two hundred years later, the idea that all human beings are born equal has taken on an altogether different meaning. From the 1960s onwards there emerged in Britain and America the serious proposition that human beings are *literally* 'born equal'. The new egalitarians will, grudgingly, admit that we are not all born physically equal (although I have spent many frustrating hours arguing with some colleagues who seek to maintain that I could have become the equal of Muhammed Ali or Lynford Christie had I put in sufficient hours of training). On mental ability, however, the new egalitarians are adamant—there are no natural differences between us. Albert Einstein, William Shakespeare, Wolfgang Amadeus Mozart and Peter Saunders all are born with identical mental capacities. The fact that some of us turn out to be better mathematicians, logicians, writers, artists or musicians than others is entirely explained by the different environmental conditions in which we were nurtured.

Let us suppose for a moment that this is true—that we are all born with equal talent and ability. If sociologists were then to discover that children born to parents occupying one social stratum tended to succeed in the occupational system much more frequently than children from another, we should not be able to explain this in terms of differential innate talents, and we should have to look elsewhere for an explanation. The obvious place to look would be at differences in motivation, effort and commitment. We would need to ask whether the more successful group of children tends (for whatever reason) to work harder than the second, whether they are more single-minded in dedicating themselves to achieving success in the occupational system while the second tends to see this as less important and is more concerned with other aspects of life, such as having a good time.

But suppose that this possibility too is ruled out. Suppose that we have good grounds for believing, not only that everybody is equally talented, but also that everybody is equally motivated in exactly the same direction. Then, and only then, would we be justified in claiming, as John Goldthorpe claims, that our society "most strikingly and incontrovertibly deviates from the ideal of genuine openness", for only then could we be sure that the competition for top jobs is skewed against certain individuals by virtue of their social background.

It is clear that the post-war tradition of social mobility research in Britain has implicitly been premised upon precisely these two assumptions—that we are all born with equal ability, and that we are all equally hard-working and committed in the pursuit of occupational success. Certainly the interpretation which John Goldthorpe places on his analysis of disparity ratios and odds ratios rests on these twin assumptions, for we have seen that, for him, the criterion of 'genuine openness' in a society is that there should be *no* association between class origins and class destinations (a disparity ratio of 1:1). This could only come about under one of two conditions. Either the occupational system would have to select individuals randomly without regard for any differences of talent and ability between them, or the pool of talented and able individuals would have to be spread equally and randomly across the class system.

The first possibility is clearly absurd. We do not and should not expect employers to take on the first individual who walks through the door, irrespective of his or her individual qualities. Occupational recruitment is and must be selective. Prospective teachers who cannot read, prospective doctors who cannot write, prospective accountants who cannot calculate percentages, such people will (hopefully!) be excluded from entry to such positions.

But if occupational recruitment is necessarily selective by ability, then Goldthorpe's insistence on a 1:1 disparity ratio can only be fulfilled if ability (and effort) are spread evenly across all social classes. This means that, on average, children born to unskilled manual worker families should be no more or less intelligent than children born to parents who work as astro-physicists. Intelligence, in other words, must not vary by social class, for if it does, then in even the most open and meritocratic society, we shall never achieve Goldthorpe's target of a 1:1 ratio.

Goldthorpe's analysis must therefore assume that intelligence is randomly distributed. But this itself then necessitates a second and even more extreme assumption: namely, that there are no innate differences of intelligence between any individuals anywhere!

The logic here is simple enough. Given that the occupational system must recruit to some extent on the basis of ability, then in any one generation we should expect to find people of higher ability tending to occupy the higher social class positions. To the extent that differences of ability are innate, this means that the children born to parents in higher class positions will tend to inherit some of the intellectual strengths enjoyed by their parents, with the result that average ability levels will vary between children from different social class backgrounds. Goldthorpe's whole analysis is, however, based on the assumption that this is not the case, for ability is assumed to be randomly distributed across the classes in each generation (i.e. it is treated as a constant). It follows from this that, to defend his approach, Goldthorpe would have to end up endorsing the radical egalitarian position that there can be no such thing as innate ability in the first place, and that all individuals are born with identical natural mental capacities. I could have been Einstein—it is only my environment which prevented it.

Once we assume that there are no innate differences between people, it becomes pointless even to consider the question of whether intelligence plays any part in shaping class destinies, and, by and large, British social mobility research has indeed chosen to ignore this question altogether. From David Glass to John Goldthorpe and Gordon Marshall, British sociologists who have investigated social mobility have claimed that class recruitment in Britain is anti-meritocratic, yet they have never bothered to check out the possible effects of differences of intelligence, or differences in levels of motivation, between the classes.[2] The British tradition of research on social mobility has been a long-running production of Hamlet in which the Prince has never been allowed to put in an appearance.

How has this extraordinary state of affairs come about? One important factor has been the dramatic shift in intellectual orthodoxy which took place in the 1960s and which has stifled free intellectual enquiry ever since. Professor Ron Dore recalls:

> I am old enough to have begun reading sociology during the fifties when ... people still took the concept of intelligence seriously ... I was also around to see the steady imposition of a taboo on such discussions in the 1960s; the banishment of such concepts as 'intelligence' from the discussion of skills and ability, the marginalization into what were generally labelled as right-wing ghettoes of psychologists such as Hans Eysenck who persisted in discussing the hereditary element in ability differences ... the acceptance of this taboo by academics has always seemed to me a sort of *traison des clercs*. It seriously impedes the careful, and socially responsible, analysis of important social problems.[3]

There has, in short, been an intellectual 'revolt against intelligence' since the 1960s which has succeeded in imposing a taboo on any attempt to take differences of intelligence into account in the analysis of class inequality and social mobility.

Before the 1960s social scientists (including sociologists) were well aware of the potential importance of intelligence in influencing educational and occupational success rates. The 11+ examination, established as a result of the 1944 Education Act, was premised on the assumption that children differ in their innate abilities and could therefore be selected for different types of secondary schooling on the basis of their intelligence, and, by the time that David Glass conducted his pioneering research in 1949, there was widespread optimism that this system would overcome the rigidities associated with the pre-war schooling system and would enable bright children from all social backgrounds to develop their talents to the full.

As time went by, however, it became clear that many more middle-class children than working-class children were passing the 11+ examination. While large numbers of bright working-class children did pass the exam and go on to benefit from a grammar school education, there emerged a growing concern that many more were also failing it due, not to lack of ability, but to disadvantages associated with their social class background. Through the 1950s and into the 1960s sociological studies began to report on an apparently huge 'wastage' of working-class talent which was variously explained by factors such as impoverished or overcrowded housing, lack of parental support for children's school work, teacher bias against children from relatively impoverished backgrounds, and the different 'linguistic codes' employed by school teachers and examiners (who used what Bernstein called an 'elaborated code') as compared with children from lower working-class backgrounds (who knew only a 'restricted code').[4] Just like Goldthorpe and Marshall a decade or two later, the British sociological establishment of the 1960s found middle-class children outperforming working-class children and deduced from this that the system itself was unfair and needed changing.

The eventual abolition of the 11+ examination in most parts of the country, and the widespread adoption of a non-selective system of comprehensive secondary education, was prompted by the belief that the system set up in 1944 had perpetuated the social class biases which it had been designed to break down. In particular, it was argued that fair and effective selection on the basis of intelligence was impossible because intelligence could not accurately be measured.

There is little doubt that 11+ was a blunt instrument for sorting out intellectual sheep and goats, and undoubtedly some bright working-class children failed when they 'should' have succeeded, while some dull middle-class children passed when they 'should' have failed. The examination tested numeracy and literacy skills, in addition to 'general intelligence' assessed by means of a verbal reasoning IQ test, and critics were undoubtedly correct to argue that, other things being equal, this tended to favour children from relatively advantaged cultural backgrounds (IQ tests based on non-verbal 'fluid ability' have been found to be less influenced by cultural background than verbal tests of 'crystallised ability', but these were never used in 11+).[5] Critics were similarly right to point out that 11+ selection disadvantaged 'late developers', that it was deliberately loaded against girls (because girls outperformed boys on average but were subjected to equal gender quotas), and that it generated unfair regional biases (because local education authorities differed markedly in the proportions of grammar school places they made available).

Having said this, however, it is also clear that the system did not misclassify substantial proportions of children as critics generally claimed. The best evidence for this comes from the work of A.H.Halsey, a colleague of John Goldthorpe's at Nuffield College, and a collaborator on Goldthorpe's social mobility project in the 1970s.

Halsey shares Goldthorpe's political values—they each describe themselves as 'ethical socialists'—and he shares with Goldthorpe an unshakeable belief that the British class system is unfair, anti-meritocratic, and biased against working-class children. Halsey's contribution to the Nuffield social mobility project consisted of an analysis of the educational backgrounds and experiences of the same 10,000 men whose occupational careers were analysed by Goldthorpe, and his results showed that those of them born into middle-class families had been proportionately over-represented in selective (state and private) secondary schools. Thus, 72 per cent of sons of 'service class' fathers had attended some form of selective secondary school as compared with only 24 per cent of sons of working-class fathers.

We have already seen, of course, that this project collected no information on either the intelligence or the motivation of these 10,000 individuals, and Halsey and his co-authors candidly admit that: "Our data do not yield measures of the complex amalgam of mind and character which would fully represent any of the possible definitions of merit."[6] In an attempt to correct for this, Halsey estimated average IQ scores for individuals from different social class backgrounds on the basis of data collected in the 1950s (when sociologists still believed that such scores meant something and were worth collecting). This produced average IQ estimates of 109 for those originating in the service class, 102 for those from intermediate class backgrounds, and 98 for those born to working-class parents. Working with these estimates, the authors then calculated the proportion of children from each class who 'should' have attended a selective school had the system been perfectly meritocratic.

The results of this exercise make interesting reading. While 72 per cent of service class sons attended selective schools, Halsey's calculations suggested that only 58 per cent should have done so. And while 24 per cent of working-class sons attended such schools, the calculations indicated that 28 per cent should have done so. How should we interpret these findings? Halsey and his co-authors apparently see these results as damning. Referring to the figures for the working-class, they suggest:

A shortfall of 4 per cent may not sound a very grave departure from meritocracy but in absolute terms it represents a very large number of working-class boys ... a total of around 6000 boys from the working-class who were denied their meritocratic due *each year*".[7]

Such a claim seems disingenuous. A shortfall of 4 per cent *is* tiny. The old 11+ system seems to have been remarkably accurate in allocating children to schooling on a meritocratic basis. Indeed, when we remember that Halsey conflates private and grammar schools in his analysis of 'selective schools' (which inevitably inflates the proportion of middle-class children who would have attended them), and that the study makes no allowance for the possibility that middle-class children may have been more motivated and hard-working (a reasonable supposition given all the sociological evidence about the importance of middle-class parental support for children's educational success), Halsey's results seem to indicate that ability was by far the most important single factor distinguishing those who succeeded under this system and those who failed, and that children's social class origins actually counted for very little.

What seems true of the process of educational selection is also true of the subsequent process of occupational selection. Using the same average IQ estimates that Halsey used, Adrian Heath has re-analysed Goldthorpe's data on social mobility patterns in an attempt to take account of the role played by differences of intelligence. He constructed a simple 'path model' which enables us to gauge the relative contribution of factors like class background, educational qualifications and IQ to shaping individuals' eventual class destinations. The relative contribution made by each factor is measured by a 'partial correlation coefficient', r, which can range between zero (no effect) and 1 (complete determination). Heath found that the strongest associations were those between IQ and educational success ($r=0.38$) and IQ and the eventual social class position achieved ($r=0.27$). The path from class background to class destination was much weaker, and this forced Heath to conclude that: "Those circumstances of birth which we can measure do not exert a very powerful constraint on ... later achievements".[8]

Given this sort of evidence, why is it that most sociologists have continued resolutely to ignore the importance of intelligence in shaping people's social class destinies? The simple answer is that they do not believe that intelligence as measured by IQ tests tells us anything of value. They deny that intelligence can accurately be measured or assessed by IQ tests, that there is any such thing as the 'general intelligence' which IQ tests claim to measure, and that individual differences in ability have any innate or biological foundation. In sum, they choose to believe that IQ is nothing more than a measure of cultural difference associated with different social classes. IQ tests, they say, are culture-bound and class-biased, and the fact that working-class children score lower on average than middle-class children means nothing in terms of differences in average levels of intelligence between the classes.

The debate over IQ is one which has stirred the passions on all sides for several decades, and there is no useful purpose in my rehearsing the arguments and the evidence in any detail all over again here.[9] The approach I shall adopt in later chapters is in any case agnostic on the question of whether IQ tests are culturally contaminated and class-biased, for in chapter 6 I shall develop an analysis which does not depend on any IQ data, and in chapters 7 and 8 I shall use IQ scores only where the possible influence of social class background can be strictly controlled.

It seems clear that some IQ tests (e.g. verbal reasoning tests measuring 'crystallised ability') are more culture-biased than others (e.g. non-verbal tests measuring 'fluid ability') because they depend upon some degree of acquired knowledge (such as language skills) in order to answer them. Of course, the ability to acquire knowledge may itself reflect differences of intelligence as much as differences in cultural backgrounds. Nevertheless, to the extent that all tests require some degree of acquired knowledge, they probably all entail some degree of cultural contamination, and this is likely to be relatively smaller in non-verbal tests (e.g. those involving recognition of common patterns in various shapes) than in verbal ones, and in tests conducted within rather than across contrasting cultures.

It is also clear that the risk of some cultural contamination should not lead us to dismiss all variations in IQ test results as solely the result of cultural differences. IQ tests, properly conducted, can and do provide a reasonable measure of what we think of as 'intelligence'. IQ, for example, correlates strongly with results of tests of other kinds of mental skills such as reading and maths (external validity), and scores on different kinds of IQ tests correlate highly with each other (internal validity). This suggests that various different kinds of measures of intellectual ability are all tending to converge on some common factor or cluster of factors. Moreover, IQ also turns out to be a good predictor of such measures as mental reaction times (e.g. the time taken to recognise which of two lines is longer), forward and backward digit span tests (the ability to repeat a sequence of numbers forwards relative to the ability to repeat the same sequence backwards), the evoked potentials of brainwaves (Eysenck records correlations as high as 0.6 between IQ scores and speed of brain waves evoked by sudden stimuli of light or sound), and positron emission topography (which finds that the brains of those with high IQs take up less glucose when solving problems than do the brains of those with low IQs). Phenomena like reaction times, brainwave potentials, and positron emissions relate directly to brain processing speed, accuracy and efficiency—factors which are thought to be central in determining intellectual capacity—and comparison of forward and backward digit spans enables us to rule out differential motivation as a possible cause of variations in test scores.[10]

IQ is not, therefore, a perfect indicator of intelligence, but it is a reasonably valid and reliable one, and it can be used to measure approximate differences in average levels of intelligence between different social groups, particularly when they live under similar cultural conditions.

But what, exactly, is it that IQ tests are measuring? There are two issues here. The first is whether intelligence is a general characteristic, measurable on a single scale, or whether it is an amalgam of many different characteristics, all unrelated to each other. The second is whether the differences in intelligence measured by IQ tests reflect innate and inborn differences in people's mental capacities, or whether they reflect mainly or even wholly the different environmental influences which have affected the way they think and reason.

IQ, like height, is measured on a single scale; it is unidimensional. This reflects the orthodox view that there is something called 'general intelligence' (g) which is reflected in several different kinds of mental ability. While it is recognised that intelligence may become manifest in many different kinds of intellectual abilities, it is assumed that abilities in one area tend to be related to those in another because they all derive from the same common source. For example, people with good spatial ability are assumed, on average, also to have good verbal ability, good mathematical ability, good logical reasoning ability, and so on, because all these abilities reflect a single general factor, g. If this is indeed the case, it then makes sense to attempt to measure overall intellectual strength on a single scale, just as we might speak of a general factor of 'athleticism' shared in common by those who are good at sprinting, those who are good at marathon running, those who are good at long jumping, and so on. If it were the case that successful sprinters were no better at jumping than those who are hopeless at running 100 metres, it would clearly make no sense to talk in general terms of 'athletic ability'. Similarly, if those who prove mentally adept at numeracy problems were left all at sea when it comes to solving verbal puzzles or spatial tests, then it would make no sense to talk of 'intelligence' as a general factor.

So is there a general intelligence factor? The issue is disputed. What is not disputed, however, is that many different kinds of mental abilities do appear to correlate with each other to a greater or lesser extent. It is not necessarily the case that any one individual with strong verbal reasoning ability will also have strong spatial ability or strong mathematical ability, but when large numbers of people are tested, we do tend to find that scores across different kinds of tasks correlate quite highly. Summarising the current state of research on this issue, Nicholas Mackintosh suggests:

> There are distinctions between tests of verbal and spatial ability, abstract reasoning and speed of information processing, but ... these tests all correlate positively with one another. It is, therefore, at best misleading to say that these tests measure wholly independent abilities. More plausibly, they measure a set of overlapping processes whose importance varies from one kind of test to another. Whether there is a single, underlying process of general intelligence that is more important than the others is simply not known.[11]

In other words, ability in one area does tend to correlate with ability in others. While this of itself does not necessarily indicate a single common factor, general intelligence, it does rule out the idea that different aspects of mental ability are randomly associated in individuals. To revert to our analogy with athletics, this is akin to saying that speed, strength, agility, and so on do not necessarily spring from the same single source, but they do tend to overlap, which means it does make sense when comparing average performance levels between different groups in the population to talk in terms of differences in general athletic ability. So too with intelligence. Intelligence may well be multi-faceted, but the various dimensions of intelligence do tend to cluster in such a way that we can reasonably talk of differences in average levels of intelligence between different groups in the population.

This conclusion inevitably leads us to the second question: To what extent is intelligence genetically or environmentally determined? To the extent that intelligence is genetic, it is clear that it will be determined by the interplay of multiple genes, each of which makes a relatively small contribution to the overall variance in mental performance within the population.[12] Similarly, to the extent that it is shaped by environmental factors, it is also clearly the case that many different influences will be involved, including intra- as well as inter-family differences in the way children are nurtured.

Like the issue of general intelligence, the question of the relative contribution to intelligence of genetics and environment is hotly contested, and again, there is no absolute and definitive answer. Two points, however, are clear. First, both genetics and environment are involved—most scientists working in this field now agree that mental capacity is to some extent determined biologically, and if this is correct, there is clearly no justification for sociologists to continue to ignore biological factors in their analysis of phenomena like social mobility. Second, genetics and environment interact in quite complex ways. Environmental influences—relations with parents, input from schools, mental exertion and practice, even a mother's diet while the foetus is still in the womb—can change our intellectual capacities and performance. Equally, our genetic inheritance can shape the kinds of environmental influences to which we are exposed. Plomin, for example, suggests that genetic dispositions often lead us into environments which accentuate our genetic propensities (e.g. people with a strong innate ability in some specific mental task often seek out tasks which utilise and therefore develop precisely this capacity). Similarly, factors which we think of as 'environmental' influences on intellectual development may themselves have a genetic component (e.g. parents who enjoy reading will encourage their children to use books, but parents who enjoy reading may do so precisely because they have a high innate verbal ability with a genetic basis which is likely to have been passed on to their children).[13]

Given that intelligence is a function of both 'nature' and 'nurture', and that these two factors are each themselves entailed in the other, it is obviously extremely difficult to parcel out their respective influences. Current research such as the Human Genome project[14] and Plomin's planned work in London analysing genotypes of 10,000 children is now seeking DNA markers identifying genes associated with various mental abilities, but the results of such work still lie some years into the future. For the moment, the best we can do is to use experimental methods to try to identify the relative contributions of nature and nurture by holding one or other constant while allowing the other to vary.

Hans Eysenck, who claims that heredity is twice as important as environment in explaining differences in intelligence, bases this estimate on the results of repeated experiments carried out over many years by many different researchers.[15] In all these experiments, the logic is essentially the same, namely, to compare variations in mental ability between people who are unrelated in their genetic inheritance but who share a common environment (e.g. children raised in children's homes) with variations between people who are genetically related but raised in contrasting environments (e.g. twins raised by different sets of foster parents). Eysenck has long been reviled by many mainstream British sociologists, and many attempts have been made to discredit his work, but the overall conclusion from the work he surveys is compelling.

The strongest experiments focus on the performance of identical (monozygotic) twins as compared with non-identical (dizygotic) twins. MZ twins share all their genes in common while DZ twins share 50 per cent of their genes. Ignoring Cyril Burt's now discredited work, and aggregating the results of other researchers working in this field, Eysenck reports the following average correlations in intelligence test scores:

* MZ twins raised in the same environment = 0.87
* MZ twins reared in separate environments = 0.77
* DZ twins raised in the same environment = 0.53.[16]

These figures compare with an average correlation of 0.23 for biologically unrelated individuals who are raised in a common environment (e.g. adopted or foster children), and with a correlation of zero for unrelated children raised in different environments.

It is clear from these figures that intelligence is not solely genetic (if it were, there would be a perfect correlation of 1.0 between scores of MZ twins, irrespective of whether or not they were raised together, and there would be a zero correlation between scores of unrelated children raised in the same environment). It is also clear, however, that there is a substantial genetic component to intelligence, for variations attributable to separate environments appear much lower than those attributable to different genetic inheritance.

Critics, such as Kamin, have attempted to dispute this conclusion by suggesting that the experimental conditions on which these results depend were often flawed. In particular, he suggests (probably rightly) that twins who are raised separately are often nevertheless brought up in similar environments, and this will tend to underestimate the contribution attributable to environmental factors because the degree of environmental variation is relatively small. In similar vein, he also suggests that studies of adopted and foster children are weakened by the fact that adoption agencies often try to place children in homes similar to those of their natural parents, thus again reducing any potential effect of environmental variation. In the end, however, such criticisms appear trifling, for Kamin and others like him cannot refute the strongest evidence from twin studies pointing to a substantial genetic component in measured intelligence. This is the evidence which demonstrates average correlations on test results of 0.77 for MZ twins reared apart as compared with 0.53 for DZ twins reared together.

If environment were more important than heredity, then the relative strength of these correlations should be reversed. Identical twins raised separately should differ more in their scores than non-identical twins raised together, for they have clearly been subjected to greater environmental variation. The opposite, however, holds true. Even when brought up separately, identical twins score much more similarly on IQ tests than non-identical twins who were kept together. Kamin accepts that the correlations reported by Eysenck are genuine, and although he quibbles with many of the other findings reported by Eysenck, he can offer no environmental explanation for this, the most crucial of them. To the extent that anything is ever proven in social science, the undisputed fact that identical twins brought up separately correlate so much more highly on test scores than non-identical twins raised together proves that intelligence is based to a substantial degree (perhaps 50 per cent, or more) on a cluster of genes which we inherit from our parents.

When it comes to intellectual ability, therefore, we are not all born equal. It is true that intelligence is difficult to measure accurately by IQ tests—but careful testing of fluid ability does enable us to measure it at a level of reliability which allows us to make fairly accurate judgements about average levels of intelligence among different groups in any given population. It is true that intelligence entails a variety of different kinds of mental capacities—but these capacities do tend to correlate with each other, which suggests that different kinds of intellectual processes are in some way related. It is true that we cannot be certain of the relative contribution made by environmental and genetic factors—but we can be certain that both make some contribution and that there is a significant biological basis to variations in measured intelligence.

For too long, those who seek to deny that there are *any* innate differences between us have focused on the difficulties and uncertainties surrounding research in this field in order to justify the spurious claim that such research should be disregarded altogether. But science rarely deals in absolute certainties, it deals in balances of probabilities. In the area of intelligence, sufficient research has been carried out over the years to demonstrate that we are not all born equal, despite the wishes of egalitarian sociologists that it were otherwise. This being the case, it is time to remove the taboo which has prevented British sociology from seriously addressing these issues, and to accept that differences of innate intelligence do exist. Having established this, we can then begin to re-examine the research findings on social mobility in a new light.

Why Intelligence Must Vary By Class
But May Not Vary By Race

W E KNOW that working-class children in Britain are three to four times less likely to achieve middle-class jobs than are children born to middle-class parents. Given that intelligence is likely to play some role in the way people are selected for jobs, the obvious question is whether working-class children are on average less intelligent than middle-class children. Could the 3:1 or 4:1 disparity ratio in relative social mobility chances be explained by a tendency for working-class parents to produce children of a lower average intelligence than middle-class parents do?

For the last twenty or thirty years British sociologists have tended to deny this possibility. They have resisted the idea because they find it offensive. It reminds them of discredited nineteenth century theories of social evolution and of twentieth century theories of eugenics, and they will have nothing to do with it. In a book of well over 300 pages, for example, John Goldthorpe takes just one paragraph to dispense with the possibility that the pattern of social mobility he has found could be explained by social class differences in average levels of intelligence. Such an explanation will, he says, appeal only to "latter-day Social Darwinists or Smilesians".[1]

Other sociologists have rejected intelligence-based theories of social mobility as 'ideological'. Pierre Bourdieu, a key figure in the sociology of education, tells us that what appear to be class differences in intelligence are 'in reality' cultural differences: "A sociological explanation can account for the unequal achievement usually imputed to unequal ability".[2] For Bourdieu, the belief that success and failure are governed by differences of ability is simply the way in which dominant classes legitimate their position:

> The *ideology of giftedness*, the cornerstone of the whole educational and social system, helps to enclose the under-privileged classes in the role which society has given them by making them see as natural inability things which are only a result of an inferior social status.[3]

Similarly, in the United States, two of the most influential writers on the American class system reassure us that the "true function" of IQ testing lies in "legitimating the social institutions underpinning the stratification system itself".[4]

Not only in sociology, but in psychology too, those who have insisted on researching differences in innate intelligence which might help explain why some social groups achieve more than others have been marginalised and persecuted. In Britain, Hans Eysenck was banned by the National Union of Students from speaking on university campuses during the 1970s, and, in the USA, Richard Herrnstein was hounded by students and colleagues alike for his views.[5] Critics in America at that time called for "a code of conduct that will discourage colleagues tempted to follow and broaden the paths of irresponsible research now trod by such psychologists as Jensen, Herrnstein and Eysenck".[6] In other words, research on such issues should not simply be ignored, but should be banned. Things have not changed much: in 1996 *The g factor*, written by an Edinburgh psychologist, Chris Brand, was withdrawn by the publisher on the grounds that it made "assertions which we find repellent".[7]

Part of the reason why writers like Herrnstein and Eysenck have attracted such vicious criticism and opposition is that they applied their ideas to racial as well as social class differences. At a time when the black movement was on the offensive in both Britain and America, and when affirmative action legislation was being passed in the United States in an attempt to 'rectify' the social disadvantages which were thought to have hindered black achievement in the schools and the occupational system, research purporting to demonstrate that blacks were, on average, less intelligent than whites was bound to provoke uproar. This whole issue of racial differences in intelligence has, of course, surfaced again recently as a result of the publication of Herrnstein and Murray's book, *The Bell Curve*, which finds that Asians are (on average) slightly more intelligent than whites who are in turn significantly more intelligent on average than blacks. The book has attracted much the same reaction as did the work of Jensen and Eysenck a generation earlier.[8]

It is not my intention here to discuss race and intelligence. This is not an issue which I have researched, and given that the ethnic minorities (Asians as well as Afro-Caribbeans) account for no more than five per cent of the British population, it is not an issue which dominates analysis of social mobility patterns in Britain in a way that it does in the USA. It is, however, an issue which has muddied the waters of debate over class and intelligence, for criticisms of research on racial differences have often been assumed to apply equally to research on class differences. There is, however, a crucial distinction to be drawn between the two.

There is no *a priori* reason to believe that average levels of intelligence *should* vary between different racial groups. They might, and they might not—it is for research to determine the question as best it can by means of empirical evidence. When we turn to consider class, however, there are good grounds for believing that such differences *should* exist. The reason for this is that race is what sociologists call an 'ascribed' social role while class is an 'achieved' social role.

To all intents and purposes, our racial identity is fixed at birth. Of course there are ambiguities, and racial identities may in this sense be 'socially negotiated'. But by and large (and the example of Michael Jackson notwithstanding), race is not something which people achieve through their own efforts, and it does not change over one's lifespan, as a result of what else we are and what we do. Clever black children do not turn white, just as clever white children do not turn Asian. If you are black and you are clever, you remain black, no matter how successful you become.

Class is very different. It is true that when we are born, we share the class identity of our parents, but this is a temporary identity, pending our own occupational fate once we leave school. In the adult population, class depends on what we have achieved, not on what we were born as. Class membership is selected and competed for in a way that racial membership is not. Given that one criterion of selection is likely to be intelligence, we should therefore expect to find brighter people moving into the middle-class in each generation. There is no such criterion of selection for race. Clever black children will remain black, but clever working-class children will not necessarily remain working-class.

To repeat, blacks may or may not be less intelligent on average than whites, but there is no logical reason to believe that this will be the case because membership of racial groups is not deliberately and consciously selected on the basis of mental ability, and individuals do not compete with each other for their racial identities. Stratification by class is, by contrast, in principle open to competition and selection, which means that those individuals with the appropriate attributes for middle-class entry (such as high intelligence) should be expected to end up there.

Research on the relation between class and IQ seems to bear this out empirically. Citing American data, Eysenck reports average IQ scores of 128 for accountants and lawyers, 122 for teachers, 109 for electricians, 96 for truck drivers and 91 for miners and farmhands. He also shows correlations as high as 0.81 between IQ scores and incomes, and 0.91 between IQ and occupational prestige (as measured by surveys of how the public ranks different jobs in terms of their social standing). In short, the occupational system does (unsurprisingly) tend to select people by measured mental ability.

There is also evidence that men and women tend to end up mating, not only with people from a similar social class, but also with partners with a similar level of IQ to their own. To the extent that intelligence is geneti-cally determined, this process of 'assortive mating' means that 'high intelligence' genes from one parent are unlikely to be counteracted by 'low intelligence' genes from the other. Put another way, intelligent women will tend, on average, to mate with intelligent men, with the result that they tend to produce intelligent children. Conversely, dull parents will tend, on average, to produce dull children [9].

Putting these two sets of evidence together, it is clear that working-class parents must be expected to produce children whose average IQ is lower than that of children born to middle-class parents. If people entering middle-class jobs tend to be more intelligent, and if they select intelligent partners, then (assuming that intelligence has some genetic basis) it must be the case that the children they produce will tend to be relatively intelligent as well. This, of course, is precisely what we find. As we saw in chapter 4, research in Britain in the 1950s recorded average IQ scores of 109 for middle-class children as compared with 98 for working-class children.

Here, then, is a clear alternative hypothesis to the one developed by Goldthorpe. For Goldthorpe, working-class children fare worse than middle-class children when they enter the occupational system because they suffer from (unspecified) social disadvantages. This is a plausible hypothesis, but it is not self-evidently the correct one. The alternative explanation is that working-class children fare worse than middle-class children because they are on average less intelligent. According to this second hypothesis, the occupational system selects people for entry in each generation on the basis of their ability, these people produce children whose ability to some extent reflects that of their parents, and these children are then in turn selected for occupational entry on the basis of their ability, which means there is a tendency for children to end up in much the same social class positions as their parents.

Both of these hypotheses are plausible, but which (if either) is correct? The evidence demonstrating a clear association between social class and IQ seems to point towards the second, but as we saw in chapter 4, IQ testing is a contentious area, and those who are predisposed to reject this kind of explanation are unlikely to be convinced by IQ data. Despite all the evidence and arguments outlined in the previous chapter, there is still among British sociologists a resolute scepticism about IQ data. Evidence that middle-class people have higher average IQ scores than working-class people is generally dismissed on the grounds that IQ tests are culturally biased in favour of those from middle-class backgrounds, and in the end, no amount of evidence and reasoning is likely to break down this belief.

At this point, debate reaches an *impasse*. On one side stand those convinced that class differences in social mobility chances are the product of the various *social advantages and disadvantages* accruing to children born into different class backgrounds (what I shall call the 'SAD' hypothesis). On the other stand those convinced that the explanation lies in average differences of intelligence between different social classes (a view which is essentially compatible with the 'meritocracy' hypothesis which holds that classes are recruited on the basis of *ability plus effort*). The first group refuses to acknowledge the validity of the key evidence on which the second group rests its case—evidence based on the results of IQ testing. The result is that each group ignores the other, each believing it is right and that the others are a bunch of non-scientific dogmatists.

It is, however, possible to break out of this intellectual cul-de-sac. To make progress, it is necessary only to accept that people do differ to some (unspecified) extent in their innate mental capacities. Some sociologists are likely to resist even this possibility and to hold fast to an extreme version of environmental determinism in which everybody is born with identical brain capacity and all differences of intellectual ability are to be explained with reference to environmental influences impacting after the moment of conception. This does not, however, appear to be the position adopted by the more sophisticated sociologists working in this field. We have already seen, for example, that A.H.Halsey, Goldthorpe's collaborator on the Nuffield social mobility project, was prepared to accept the possibility of genetically-based differences in ability, and in a recent publication, Gordon Marshall too has accepted that it is not inconceivable that "middle-class parents pass on to their children, whether genetically or environmentally ... talents ... such as intelligence and motivation", although he chooses not to analyse this possibility on the grounds that he is "not qualified to pursue the biological aspects of this argument".[10]

To those who continue to rule out the possibility of any innate differences between individuals, we must at this point bid *adieu*. There is no more to be said to them, and they can safely be left in their academic ghettoes, doomed forever to search for convincing explanations of individual success and failure which look everywhere except at individuals themselves. To those of a more open mind, however, we may extend an invitation to climb aboard an exciting intellectual roller-coaster which starts with the imagination and ends up in a journey through a hitherto unexplored terrain of new empirical evidence.

What Would a Perfect Meritocracy Look Like?

W E HAVE seen that, for Goldthorpe, a perfect meritocracy would be achieved only when the disparity ratios between working-class and middle-class chances of success or failure in the occupational class system shrank to unity. We have also seen, however, that this is an unrealistic criterion to impose since recruitment in a meritocratic system will depend partly on intelligence. In a pure meritocracy, 'bright' people will rise to the higher positions, and because bright people will tend to produce bright children, there will be a tendency for the children of the middle-classes to outperform the children of the working-class.

The question, therefore, is how big a disparity between the classes should we expect to find in a purely meritocratic system? Bigger, certainly, than Goldthorpe's criterion of 1:1, but would it be as great as the disparity ratios of 3:1 or 4:1 which he reports from his study of social mobility among males in Britain?

To answer this, we can construct from Goldthorpe's own data a model of social mobility in a pure meritocracy. Five points need to be emphasised at the outset.

First, nothing in this chapter should be taken to imply that Britain *is* a meritocracy. The point of the exercise is to establish the pattern of social mobility which *would* exist if it *were* a meritocratic society, for this will then enable us to compare the reality (as reported by Goldthorpe's research) with the (imaginary) 'perfect' model in order to gauge the extent to which the reality falls short of the ideal.

Second, it needs to be emphasised that the model does not depend on IQ test results. To accept the model, it is necessary only to accept that individuals differ to some extent in their innate intellectual abilities, and that the distribution of such abilities within the population is approximately 'normal' (i.e. most people cluster around the average ability level with proportionately fewer at each extreme—Figure 1 gives an example of a variable which is normally distributed).[1] Having accepted this proposition, we can leave on one side the practical question of how and whether such differences could be tested and measured, for we are here constructing an imaginary world, and in such a world we need not be distracted by technical problems about how we are to measure such abilities. In what follows, I shall be deducing theoretical IQ scores rather than inserting real, measured scores into the model, and in this way, we can avoid all the arguments about whether or not actual IQ testing in practice successfully measures ability.

Figure 1: A Hypothetical Normal Distribution

```
                           x
                          xxx
                         xxxxx
                        xxxxxxxxx
                      xxxxxxxxxxxxxxx
                    xxxxxxxxxxxxxxxxxxxxx
                 xxxxxxxxxxxxxxxxxxxxxxxxxxxxx
          xxxxxxxxxxxxxxxxxxxxxxxxxxxxxxxxxxxxxxxxx
      01_____*_____ 35
```

In this example, there are 91 observations (each denoted by 'x') distributed on a range from score 1 (on the extreme left hand side) to score 35 (on the extreme right hand side). Most observations cluster around the middle of the distribution, with a tailing off towards each of the extremes. The asterisk (*) marks the arithmetic average (the mean), which in a normally distributed variable is also the mode (the point at which more cases cluster than at any other point). In this example, the mean score is 18, and this is also the score representing the maximum number of observations (7 in this example).

Third, the model we are about to construct will take the social class positions and the theoretically-deduced IQ scores of fathers as representing the social class and IQ scores of both parents. This is partly for the sake of simplicity and partly because Goldthorpe's data relate only to males. In reality, of course, fathers and mothers may occupy different class positions and may have different intellectual abilities (although we have seen that 'assortive mating' tends to compress such variations). We shall assume, however, that the number of cases where fathers score 'higher' than mothers is balanced by the number of cases where the reverse is the case so that these differences will cancel each other out.

Fourth, we shall (again for the sake of simplicity) ignore the 'intermediate classes' and focus entirely on the rates of interchange which should be expected between working-class and 'service class' origins and destinations, for it is here that Goldthorpe reports the most extreme disparity ratios.

Fifth, we shall leave aside for the moment the second element in the theory of meritocracy, namely 'effort', and shall concentrate solely on ability. In fact, as we shall see, the way we shall deduce hypothetical IQ scores could be extended to encompass hypothetical motivation scores as well, provided only that both of these attributes are normally distributed in the population. At this stage, however, it is important to keep things simple.

The *first step* in constructing the model is to focus on the older of two generations. In Goldthorpe's research, he compared fathers and sons, so let us concentrate on the fathers in his sample. We know from Goldthorpe's data that, in the fathers' generation, just 14.3 per cent occupied 'service class' (i.e. middle-class) positions while 54.8 per cent were in working-class positions (the remainder were in intermediate positions which we shall ignore). Under conditions of a perfect meritocracy, these fathers would have been recruited to their occupational class positions purely on the basis of their ability (remember that we are ignoring 'effort' for the time being). Thus, had a perfect meritocracy been operating, we can say that all of the fathers who made it to the service class would have been in the top 14 per cent of the ability distribution in their generation, and that all of the fathers who entered the working-class would have been in the bottom 55 per cent of this distribution.

For the sake of convenience, these proportions can be translated into IQ scores. The scale of IQ is normally distributed with a mean (average) score of 100 and a standard deviation of 15 (the 'standard deviation' expresses the average absolute amount by which any one person selected at random is likely to differ from the mean score). From this, we can calculate that the top 14 per cent of the ability distribution should all score 116 or higher on IQ tests while the bottom 55 per cent should all score 102 or lower. Put another way, in a perfect meritocracy, all of the service class fathers would have had an IQ of 116 or better, and all the working-class fathers would have had an IQ no higher than 102.

Note that I am not suggesting that IQ tests are in reality this accurate—in the real world, there are doubtless cases where people in the top 14 per cent of the ability range would not score this high on IQ tests, just as some of those in the bottom 55 per cent of the ability range would not score this low. IQ tests are not perfect measures, which is precisely why this model deduces what the scores should be rather than depending on data from actual test results. Throughout these calculations, we are here deducing the IQ scores which people *should* achieve given their ability, and these calculations do not depend for their accuracy on how well people actually perform in such tests in the real world. Issues of culture-bias, and other such criticisms made against the use of IQ data, do not therefore apply to the model which we are constructing.

The *second step* in this model is to develop the same calculations for the sons' generation. Goldthorpe's data tell us that, in the sons' generation, 26.5 per cent were in service class jobs while 43.8 per cent were in the working-class. The substantial difference between the size of these classes in each of the two generations is explained by the expansion of middle-class employment and the contraction in working-class employment during the intervening period—as we saw in chapter 3, economic growth in the twentieth century has expanded the amount of 'room at the top' of the occupational class system. It follows from these figures that, had the sons been recruited to their jobs purely on meritocratic criteria, the top 27 per cent of the ability distribution would have ended up in the service class and the bottom 44 per cent would have gravitated to the working-class. Translated into pure IQ scores, this means that sons entering the service class should all have had an IQ of 109 or higher, while those entering the working-class would have had an IQ at or below 98.

So far, so good! The *third step* in the model is the most crucial, for this involves calculating the statistical probabilities of sons ending up in the same social class as their fathers if occupational placement in both generations took place purely on the basis of intelligence. How likely is it, for example, that middle-class fathers with an IQ of 116 or more would produce sons with an IQ of 109 or more (the minimum score necessary if they are to follow in their fathers' footsteps)?

To answer this question, we need to estimate the correlation between fathers' IQ scores and those of their sons. To understand why this estimation has to be made, and how it might reasonably be made, it is necessary to understand something of the principles behind what statisticians refer to as *regression to the mean*.

Figure 2: A Hypothetical Example of a Plot of Parents'
IQ Scores against Children's IQ Scores with a Correlation of Zero

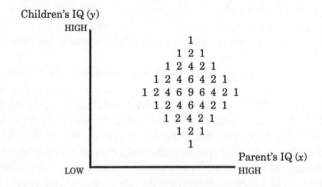

In this example, IQ scores of 105 pairs of parents and children are plotted against each other. Scores in both generations are normally distributed and extend over the same range. With a zero correlation between them, children's scores are distributed independently of those of their parents and tend to cluster around the mean of 100 forming a 3-dimensional bell shape.

Let us think about this first in common sense terms. Suppose there were no correlation between the IQ scores of parents (variable x) and those of their children (variable y). This would imply that IQ is uninfluenced by both genetics and environment—an unrealistic assumption but let that pass for the purposes of exposition. In such a situation, knowing the IQ of the parent (the value of x) would not help at all in predicting the IQ of the child (the value of y)—the two scores would vary at random. The best prediction we could make of the child's IQ under these conditions would be to equate it with the average score of y, an IQ of 100, for more children score 100 than any other score.[2] With no correlation between scores of parents and children, therefore, parents with an IQ of 140 would be just as likely as parents with an IQ of 60 to produce a child with an IQ of 100, and this would be the most likely outcome in both cases. If we were to plot on a graph the scores of x against the scores of y, we would find that, for any value of x, more cases fell on the mean of y (35 out of 105 in figure 2) than on any other point on the graph. The best-fitting straight line (what statisticians call the 'least squares regression line') which we would be able to draw in this situation would therefore be a horizontal line through the mean value on the y axis (i.e. an IQ score of 100). Put in statistical terminology, a zero correlation between two normally distributed variables thus entails a maximum 'regression to the mean'.

Now consider the opposite extreme case, where parents' IQ scores correlate exactly with the scores achieved by their children (this, of course, is just as unrealistic as the first scenario). In this situation, knowing the IQ of the parent (the value of x) would enable us to make 100 per cent accurate predictions of the IQ of the child (the value of y). Plotted on a graph, every point would fall on a straight line drawn at 45 degrees through the origin of the two axes. From this line, we could read off the value of y for each value of x—a parent with an IQ of 140 would produce a child with an IQ of 140, a parent with an IQ of 60 would produce a child with an IQ of 60, and so on. As in the first example, the mean IQ score of both parents and children would be 100, but there would be no regression to this mean. In both examples, more children score 100 than any other single score, but in this second case, all of those scoring 100 would have parents who also scored 100.

Figure 3: A Hypothetical Plot of Parents' IQ Scores
against Children's IQ Scores with a Correlation of 1.0

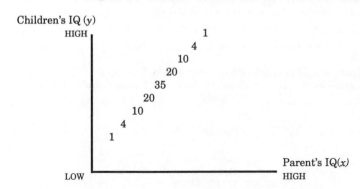

In this example, IQ scores of 105 pairs of parents and children are again plotted against each other. Again, scores are normally distributed over the same range in each generation, but, this time, children's scores are identical to those of their parents. With a perfect correlation between children's IQ scores and those of their parents, every observation now falls on a 45 degree straight line forming a cross-section through a bell shape. There is no regression to the mean.

It should be clear from these two examples that, wherever we find a correlation between two normally distributed variables which is less than one, there will be a regression to the mean. Put in simple terms, this means that cases which register extreme scores on X will tend to register less extreme scores on Y, and that extreme scores on Y will tend to relate to cases with a less extreme score on X. The phenomenon is simply illustrated with reference to height. Tall parents tend to produce tall children, but the correlation between parents' and children's heights is less than 1. This means that, if we were to measure the heights of children born to the tallest 10 per cent of parents, we would find that some of them fail to be included among the tallest 10 per cent of their generation and that some of those among the tallest 10 per cent of children will have parents who were not themselves in this first decile in their own generation. Most of the children born to the tallest parents will still be tall, but their average height (adjusted or 'standardised' to take account of any overall change in average heights between the two generations) will have fallen as compared with that of their parents.

The same phenomenon has been documented in the case of IQ. Eysenck cites work by Terman on a sample of 1528 exceptionally intelligent individuals, all of whom had an IQ of 140 or more, and whose average IQ score was 152.[3] Most mated with partners who also had a high IQ (average 125) producing a set of parents with an average IQ of 138.5. When their children were tested, however, the average IQ score was somewhat lower than this at 133.2. There had, in other words, been some regression to the mean. Similarly, Waller has found that middle-class parents achieve average IQ scores of 114 while their children register a lower average of 109. Similarly, unskilled manual worker parents have an average IQ of 81 while their children score an average of 91.[4] Again, we see here evidence of regression to the mean: some children of bright parents are less than bright, some children of average parents turn out to be bright, and so on. This is illustrated by a hypothetical example in Figure 4.

Figure 4: A Hypothetical Illustration of a Tendency
Towards Regression to the Mean between IQ Scores of Parents and Children

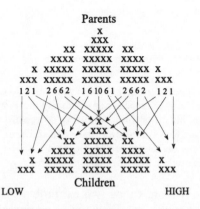

In this example, IQ scores of 64 pairs of parents and children are correlated at less than 1 which entails a regression to the mean because some dull parents have brighter children, and some bright parents have duller ones. The illustration is taken from H.Eysenck, *The Inequality of Man*, p. 131.

It is important to understand that regression to the mean, of itself, tells us nothing about the relative contributions of heredity and environment in the determination of intelligence. Eysenck seems to have become somewhat confused on this point, for he suggests that regression to the mean in IQ scores of children as compared with their parents is consistent with a genetic theory of intelligence but is inconsistent with an environmental one. His reasoning is that children inherit a mix of different genes from each parent, which tends to reduce the likelihood of extreme characteristics such as exceptionally high or low intelligence being replicated (thus we will expect to find regression to the mean in IQ scores). If IQ were environmentally determined, by contrast, he suggests that this would reinforce rather than weaken the transmission of parental characteristics, for high IQ parents will provide a stimulating intellectual environment which should generate IQ scores in their children even higher than their own (i.e. a result which he takes to be inconsistent with regression to the mean). Eysenck's argument is, however, fallacious, for we shall find regression to the mean wherever there is a correlation of less than 1 between two normally distributed variables. Regression, in other words, is a function of a less than perfect correlation, and it tells us nothing about the way different factors (such as nature and nurture) may be influencing this correlation.

Where Eysenck is right, however, is in pointing out that regression to the mean will ensure high rates of social mobility in an open social system in which occupational recruitment takes place on the basis of intelligence. It has often been suggested that class positions in a truly meritocratic society would increasingly be inherited since bright parents in the top classes will produce bright children who will themselves then enter the top classes, and so on down the generations. This reasoning seems to have informed Herrnstein's conclusion that inheritance of social positions will increase, the more meritocratic a society becomes. It was also the logic behind Halsey's early attempt at modelling social mobility in a pure meritocracy in which he suggested that only just over one per cent of the children of a less intelligent lower class would achieve upward mobility in each generation.[5]

The argument, however, is false, for it assumes a virtually perfect correlation between the IQ of parents and that of their children (with a correlation of 1, there is no regression to the mean). Put in everyday language, these gloomy scenarios forget that, while bright parents tend to produce bright children, not all their children will be bright (the correlation is above 0 but less than 1), which means that, on average, the IQ of their children will be lower than that of the parents, and, in a perfect meritocracy, downward mobility will be the result (the reverse, of course, is also true for children born to dull parents). As Eysenck puts it: "Regression is intimately connected with social mobility ... Regression mixes up the social classes, ensures social mobility and favours meritocracy."[6]

In constructing a model of expected social mobility patterns in a perfect meritocracy, it is therefore necessary to impute a correlation between parents' and children's IQ scores. In the present case, we shall assume a correlation of 0.5. There are two good reasons for building this assumption into the model.

First, according to Herrnstein, this is roughly the correlation which would be expected if IQ were based wholly on innate (genetic) intelligence.[7] Second, a correlation in IQ scores of 0.5 is implied by data on the association between social class and IQ cited by Eysenck.[8] By settling on an imputed correlation between parents' and children's IQ of 0.5, we are therefore constructing a model consistent with a strong version of the genetic theory of intelligence, and which assumes that Eysenck's data on class and IQ are accurate. If these assumptions are unwarranted and the correlation is actually very different from 0.5, then this will show up when we come to compare our model with the actual data on social mobility rates taken from Goldthorpe's survey—i.e. the model will not fit. If this happens, then we shall be forced to conclude, either that intelligence cannot predict social mobility, or that Herrnstein and Eysenck are wrong in the assumptions they make about the links between parental social class, parental IQ, and children's IQ.

Having settled on a correlation coefficient of 0.5, it is now possible to move on to the *fourth step* in constructing our model in which we calculate from the expected regression to the mean the proportion of children from each social class who would end up in various different class locations under conditions of perfect meritocracy. Four patterns have to be established:

(a) Middle-Class Children Eligible For Middle-Class Entry

We calculated earlier that, had they been recruited purely on the basis of intelligence, the middle-class fathers in Goldthorpe's survey should all have had an IQ of 116 or above. We also saw that the expansion of the middle-class has meant that, for the sons of these fathers, the IQ threshold for middle-class entry would have fallen to 109. Assuming a correlation of 0.5 between parents' and children's IQ scores, we can calculate that 59 per cent of children produced by parents with an IQ of 116 or more would have an IQ of 109 or above. A model of social mobility under conditions of perfect meritocracy would therefore predict that 59 per cent of the children born into the middle-class will be bright enough to stay there.

(b) Middle-Class Children Eligible Only For Working-Class Entry

In the sons' generation, we calculated earlier that only those with an IQ of 98 or less would enter the working-class, assuming purely meritocratic recruitment. What is the probability of parents with an IQ of 116 or more producing children with an IQ of 98 or less? Assuming a correlation on IQ scores of 0.5, the answer is that 21 per cent of the children of these parents would score this low. Our model of perfect meritocracy therefore predicts that 21 per cent of the sons of middle-class fathers would end up in working-class jobs.

(c) Working-Class Children Eligible For Middle-Class Entry

We saw earlier that working-class fathers would all have had an IQ of 102 or less if they had been recruited to their class positions purely on the basis of ability. Given an IQ threshhold of 109 for entry into the middle-class in the sons' generation, we can calculate that 18 per cent of the sons of these fathers would have an IQ high enough to qualify.

(d) Working-Class Children Eligible Only For Working-Class Entry

The upper IQ limit for entry into the working-class in the sons' generation is 98. Of those born to parents with an IQ no higher than 102, 58 per cent would be predicted to have an IQ of 98 or less. Our model therefore predicts that, under conditions of perfect meritocracy, 58 per cent of the children born to working-class parents will remain in the working-class.

Having calculated all the predicted class destinations of children born to middle-class and working-class parents, the model can now be compared with the actual pattern of social mobility between these two classes recorded by Goldthorpe's 1972 survey (Table 1 p. 46).

This table reveals an extraordinarily high degree of fit between Goldthorpe's findings and a model of perfect meritocracy. With the sole exception of downward mobility from the middle-class into the working-class (where the actual rate of movement is about 25 per cent less than that predicted), the model fits Goldthorpe's data almost exactly. The social mobility histories of the ten thousand men interviewed for Goldthorpe's study in 1972 are almost precisely what we would have expected to find had they and their fathers been recruited to their class positions purely on the basis of their intelligence.

The implications of this finding can hardly be exaggerated. Rarely in social science are we able to develop simple models which fit the empirical evidence so closely. What Table 1 (p. 46) tells us is that, assuming only that intelligence is normally distributed in the population, and that there is a correlation of 0.5 between the intelligence of parents and that of their children, then existing patterns of social mobility in Britain correspond almost exactly with the patterns which would be found if class recruitment were based solely on differences of intelligence between individuals.

Where does this leave Goldthorpe, Marshall, and all the other sociologists down the years who have so confidently claimed that social mobility has little or nothing to do with intelligence? Goldthorpe, remember, simply asserted that a disparity ratio as high as 4:1 could not possibly be the product of differences in average levels of intelligence between the classes, yet we now see that this is precisely the sort of ratio which we should expect to find if class recruitment were based solely on innate intelligence!

Once we allow for the differences in average levels of intelligence which would exist between classes recruited on meritocratic principles, we find that what Goldthorpe described as the 'gross' advantages enjoyed by middle-class children in Britain all but disappear. Goldthorpe's 4:1 disparity ratio in favour of those born into the middle-class compares with an advantage when allowance is made for transmission of intelligence across the generations of just 1.4:1 in favour of the middle-class child avoiding a working-class destination, and no advantage at all when considering the relative chances of children from different backgrounds entering the middle-class. Once we take account of ability differences, in other words, we end up at or very close to Goldthorpe's own criterion of social fairness, a disparity ratio of 1:1.

Clearly, Goldthorpe's claim that his evidence on relative mobility rates disproves the meritocracy hypothesis must now be rejected. His evidence is entirely consistent with the argument that people end up in the class positions to which their ability entitles them.

This does not mean that the meritocracy thesis has been proven, only that it remains plausible and has not been disproved by studies such as Goldthorpe's. The fact that our model of a perfect meritocracy is remarkably consistent with the data on social mobility does not mean that the model is necessarily the 'correct' one for interpreting these data. This is because the assumptions which we made in developing the model of perfect meritocracy might also be made in developing other models which would also, then, fit the data. Suppose, for example, that we believe that it is people's accents which determine where they end up in the class system. Provided we could convincingly argue (a) that accents are measurable on a scale from, say, 'very rough' (scored, perhaps, at 50) to 'very polished' (scored, say, at 150), (b) that accents are normally distributed (with a mean of 100 and a standard deviation of about 15) so that most people fall somewhere around the middle of the scale, and (c) that the accents of parents correlate at around 0.5 with the accents of their children, then we could retrace the steps taken in constructing the model of social mobility in a perfect meritocracy to create an equivalent model of social mobility based on the predicted distribution of people's accents. Nothing in this chapter, in other words, demonstrates that it is intelligence, and intelligence alone, which is driving patterns of social mobility. All we have demonstrated is that these patterns are almost certainly being produced by some factor or cluster of factors which is normally distributed and correlated as between parents and their children. Intelligence fits the bill, but so too might other things which we have not considered in this chapter (including, of course, motivation, the other pillar of the meritocracy thesis).

All that can be concluded at this stage, therefore, is that intelligence cannot be ruled out. But this is a substantial conclusion to reach given the history of research on social mobility in Britain. It means that the meritocracy thesis is wholly consistent with the evidence on social mobility, despite the claims of Professors Bottomore, Miliband, Worsley, Giddens, Westergaard, Scase, Goldthorpe, Marshall and many others that it is not. It also means that British sociologists must now be obliged to address the possibility that we do, after all, live in a broadly meritocratic society.

Six or seven years ago I first suggested that a left-wing political bias was blinding many British sociologists to the possibility that the class system was basically meritocratic. My argument was widely dismissed and derided at the time, and I was accused of pursuing my own, rather nasty, right-wing agenda. Ray Pawson summed up the general consensus when he commended his fellow sociologists for their "considerable restraint under a contemptible attack" from what he described as my "new right" position. "In out-arguing Saunders's case," he said, "they have shown the New Right the door".[9]

Leaving aside the curious assumption that it is necessarily 'right-wing' to suggest that we may be living in a genuine meritocracy, it is now clear that my arguments were dismissed too cavalierly. Far from being 'contemptible', my accusations appear to have been justified, and far from being 'out-argued', I have demonstrated that British sociologists have a serious case to answer. The meritocracy thesis *is* consistent with Goldthorpe's own evidence, and sociologists *have* been wrong all these years to assume that evidence of middle-class children outperforming working-class children could not possibly be explained by differential intelligence or motivation.

The analysis in this chapter has demonstrated the plausibility of the claim that social mobility patterns in Britain might be explained in terms of the operation of a genuine meritocracy. The question still remains, however: is this *really* the explanation?

Table 1
A Comparison of Actual Rates of Social Mobility with the Rates Predicted by a Model of Perfect Meritocracy

Mobility Pattern	Predicted %	Actual %
Middle-Class > Middle-Class	59	59
Middle-Class > Working-Class	21	15
Working-Class > Middle-Class	18	16
Working-Class > Working-Class	58	57

Actual figures are taken from Goldthorpe's 1972 data coded according to his original class schema, taken from Table 9.8. 'Middle-class' here refers to what Goldthorpe terms the 'service class'.

Is Britain a Meritocracy?

IN THE week of the 3rd to the 9th March, 1958, 17,414 births through-out Britain were recorded and logged as part of a huge and unique research project designed to collect information about the children's health, education, and development. The researchers have tried their best to stay in contact with all of these children ever since, and on five occasions they have revisited them (and, where appropriate, their parents, their schools and their eventual partners) and further documented the development of their lives. The last time they were interviewed was in 1991, when they were aged 33, and by then there were still 11,397 of the original panel of individuals on whom at least some information was obtained.

This National Child Development Study (NCDS) can provide us with an invaluable source of information on social mobility patterns in Britain in the recent period. Since 1958, it has recorded information on the occupations of the parents of panel members, these parents' behaviour and attitudes in relation to their children as they were raising them, the housing conditions in which the children were raised, their schooling and examination records, their measured ability at 7, 11 and 16, the employment histories of the panel members since leaving school, their attitudes to work and employment, their aspirations through childhood and adulthood, and so on. It therefore enables us to evaluate what I have called the *SAD hypothesis* (that social advantages and disadvantages determine where people end up in the class system) against the *meritocracy hypothesis* (that individual ability plus effort are the key determinants of occupational success or failure), for it includes robust and reliable information on virtually all the relevant factors entailed in each of these theories.

Because it targeted every child born in that one week in 1958, the NCDS provides us with a reliable and fairly representative survey of this age cohort. Panel 'wastage' has reduced the total size of the sample substantially, and proportionately more individuals from lower class origins have dropped out, thereby skewing the sample towards the middle-class both in terms of class origins and class destinations.[1] The surviving NCDS panel in 1991 is, therefore, no longer fully representative of all 33 year-olds in Britain, but there are still sufficient cases remaining in all classes to enable us to analyse the factors driving upward and downward social mobility. Furthermore, now that panel members have reached age 33, it is possible for the first time to take their current class position as a reasonable indicator of their eventual class of destination, although some movement between classes will obviously continue to take place in the future.

Many of the surviving panel members were not in full-time employment in 1991. These people will be omitted from the analysis which follows because they cannot be allocated to a particular social class position on the basis of their own current occupation. Dropping these cases, most of whom are part-time employees (45 per cent), 'housewives' (37 per cent) or unemployed (10 per cent), leaves us with 6,795 individuals, 85 per cent of whom are employees and 15 per cent self-employed. Because more women than men are to be found in part-time employment or in full-time housework, a disproportionate number of women have been dropped from the analysis, and this final sample consists of 70 per cent males and 30 per cent females.

All of these individuals can be classified to a 'social class' position using the system of classification developed by the Office of Population Censuses and Surveys (OPCS). For the purposes of this analysis, we shall divide them between three principal classes which we shall term the 'middle-class' (classes I and II, comprising professionals, managers, administrators and employers), the 'lower working-class' (classes IV and V, comprising semi- and unskilled manual workers), and the 'intermediate classes' (classes IIIN and IIIM, comprising mainly routine white-collar and skilled manual workers).

On this three-class schema, 52 per cent of the NCDS panel had been inter-generationally mobile (i.e. they occupied a different class position in 1991 than the one occupied by their parents in 1974 when the panel members reached the legal working age of 16). This figure is the same whether we compare the social class they had achieved by age 33 with the social class of their fathers, or with the higher social class of either the mother or the father. Table 2 (p. 59) shows that over one-third of middle-class children had been downwardly mobile, most of them into class III. Among lower working-class children, one-quarter had been upwardly mobile into the middle-class while half had moved into class III. Less than half of those achieving middle-class entry had come from middle-class origins, and less than one-third of those entering class IV/V had started out there. These *absolute* patterns are broadly consistent with those reported in previous British studies of social mobility, including Goldthorpe's which similarly found that around half of the population had undergone social mobility.

The NCDS data appear rather less consistent with Goldthorpe's results, however, when we consider *relative* measures of social mobility. Goldthorpe, it will be recalled, recorded disparity ratios in favour of middle-class children of between 3:1 and 4:1 , but Table 3 (p. 59) shows that, in the NCDS sample, children born to middle-class fathers were only about twice as likely to have achieved middle-class positions by the age of 33 as compared with children born to fathers in semi- or unskilled occupations. Does this mean that the class system has become more fluid since Goldthorpe did his research?

We need to be cautious about this. One problem is that Goldthorpe's social class categories are defined rather differently from the OPCS class categories. His definition of what he calls the 'service class' does not coincide exactly with classes I and II in the OPCS schema, and his definition of the 'working-class' is much broader than (though certainly encompasses) OPCS classes IV and V. This means that Goldthorpe's results cannot be directly compared with the NCDS findings. Furthermore, although the disparity ratio in the NCDS data is much lower than Gold-thorpe's as regards children's relative chances of achieving a middle-class position, it is broadly similar to Goldthorpe's as regards relative chances of avoiding a lower class position (around 3.5:1). If fluidity has increased, it seems that top positions have become more open but that middle-class chances of dramatic failure have not risen. We also need to remember that Goldthorpe's study focused solely on men whereas the data in Table 3 include both men and women. When women are excluded from these calculations, the advantage for middle-class children in getting into class I/II is stretched somewhat to 2.6:1, and their advantage in avoiding class IV/V also increases slightly to 3.8, thus bringing the results somewhat closer to Goldthorpe's.

Bearing all these points in mind, it is nevertheless striking that the disparity ratios for the NCDS sample are so small (particularly given our tight definition of the 'working-class' as comprising only semi- and unskilled manual workers). It will be remembered that Goldthorpe's 1972 data gave disparity ratios of around 4:1 while his 1983 data gave disparity ratios of nearer 3:1. It is not unreasonable to suggest that the NCDS disparity ratio of little more than 2:1 indicates that this trend towards greater fluidity has continued. Of particular relevance here is the fact that everybody in the NCDS sample is the same age (33 in 1991) whereas both of Goldthorpe's earlier samples were of mixed age groups. What NCDS gives us is a panel of young Britons all born and raised in the post-war years, whereas Goldthorpe's samples included men who grew up before the war. If the class system has become more fluid, we should expect this to show up particularly sharply in the NCDS sample, as indeed it does. For all these reasons, we may tentatively conclude that the increased social fluidity discovered by John Goldthorpe between 1972 and 1983 has continued to rise into the 1990s.

At ages 7, 11 and 16, the children in the NCDS survey all sat maths and English tests, and at 11 they also took a (non-standardised) general ability test consisting of eighty verbal and non-verbal items. Analysis of scores on this general ability test reveals two important findings (Table 4, p. 59). First, the children's scores reflected to some extent the social class of their parents. We can see that there was a clear and consistent gradient in mean (i.e. average) test scores between those with fathers or mothers in class I/II and those whose parents were in classes IV and V. We also see that parental class and children's test scores correlate with a coefficient (r) of 0.24. The strength of association between two variables can be expressed on a scale from 0, which indicates no association, to 1, which indicates that the first variable totally predicts the second. A correlation coefficient of 0.24 therefore indicates that the parents' class and the children's test scores are related, though not particularly strongly.

Both the SAD and the meritocracy hypotheses would expect to discover a correlation like this. For the former, it is the result of social advantages which enable middle-class children to 'over-achieve' on ability tests. For the latter, it is evidence that bright middle-class parents tend to produce and raise bright children while less bright working-class parents tend to produce and raise children of lower average ability.

The second key finding is that test scores correlate much more strongly ($r=0.37$) with the social class achieved by the children twenty-two years after taking the test, than with the class of their parents around the time that they sat it. Again, there is a clear gradient in scores ranging from those entering class I/II to those entering class IV/V, but the higher correlation is due mainly to a much more marked association between ability and class of destination at the lower end of the class hierarchy.

This result is consistent with the meritocracy thesis, but not with the SAD thesis. In a meritocratic class system we would expect bright parents often to produce bright children, but we know (and can calculate from regression to the mean) that some bright parents will produce dull children just as some dull parents will produce bright ones. Because a meritocratic class system will select able children for higher positions regardless of their social background, the association between class of origin and ability should be weaker than that between ability and class of destination, and this is indeed what we find. The particularly strong association between low ability and low class destinations indicates that bright children are tending to avoid class IV/V entry and are to some extent being selected for higher positions. The SAD hypothesis, by contrast, would predict associations of equal strength since ability is seen merely as a correlate of class background and should not itself contribute to the determination of class of destination.

It seems that ability does play some part in influencing class destinations. But could social class differences in ability alone account for the disparity ratios found in mobility tables in both the Goldthorpe and the NCDS data?

By age 33, 43 per cent of the NCDS sample were in class I/II occupations. The score achieved on the ability test by the top 43 per cent of children was 49 or above. If class positions achieved by age 33 simply reflected ability as measured at age 11, then we would expect all those achieving class I/II positions to have scored 49 or better on the ability test.

Taking an ability score of 49 as the threshold for class I/II entry, we actually find that only 62 per cent of those entering class I/II scored this highly. Put crudely, 38 per cent of those arriving in class I/II were not bright enough to be there! Here we have the first indication that class destinations have to be explained by something more than just ability. Focusing on the less able entrants to class I/II (i.e. those scoring less than 49), we find that twice as many (32 per cent) came from class I/II backgrounds as from class IV/V backgrounds (17 per cent). Looking at the data in a different way, and focusing on the lowest quartile of ability across the whole sample, we find that 41 per cent of low ability children from class I/II origins still managed to gain entry to class I/II as compared with 21 per cent of low ability children from class IV/V origins. Low ability middle-class children are therefore twice as likely to succeed as low ability children from semi- and unskilled manual worker homes, although even among the latter, around one-fifth still arrive in the middle-class despite low ability scores at age 11. It is clear from this that low ability is not necessarily a barrier to later occupational success. Conversely, high ability does appear to offer a reasonable guarantee against failure, for only 5 per cent of children in the top ability quartile ended up in class IV/V while 65 per cent of them made it to class I/II.

Ability, then, is part of the explanation for why middle-class children are more successful than working-class children, but it is not the full story. We can gauge how important it is by calculating a modified set of disparity ratios dividing the sample into those with an ability score high enough to warrant entry to class I/II and those scoring below this threshold point (Table 5 p. 60). The first part of Table 5 shows (first cell) that the relative advantage enjoyed by class I/II children over class IV/V children in achieving a middle-class destination is reduced to just 1.7:1 once we control for ability. The second part of Table 5 shows (last cell) that middle-class children reduce their relative chances of avoiding class IV/V from 3.5:1 to 2.3:1 once we control for ability. Summarising all this, it seems that differences in average ability levels between children of different classes explain anything up to a half of the disparity in their relative chances of achieving middle-class entry and avoiding lower working-class entry.

Ability is only one part of the meritocracy thesis. The other key element is 'effort' which involves both the desire to succeed and a commitment to behaviour (e.g. hard work) which is thought likely to bring success. In a meritocratic society, bright individuals will only succeed if they are motivated to do so, and people of lesser ability may still achieve relatively high positions if they are committed, motivated and hard-working. A rigorous test of the meritocracy thesis thus requires adequate measures of effort as well as ability.

In the NCDS survey, there are various possible indicators of 'effort'. From among these we shall examine (a) a 32-point motivation scale based on attitude questions answered by the children at age 16 (MOTIVATION); (b) an 'absenteeism' factor based on school truancy records and reports of trivial absences (ABSENTEEISM); and (c) a 'job commitment' factor based on answers to three attitude questions at age 33 (WORK ATTITUDES). Taken together with the ability scores (between 0 and 80) at age 11 (ABILITY TEST SCORE), these represent the major indicators for testing the meritocracy thesis.

What, then, are the comparable indicators for evaluating the SAD thesis? One, clearly, is parental class (PARENTAL CLASS) which is measured on a 3-point scale and which refers to the social class of father or mother when the child was aged 16, whichever is the higher. Linked to this is the educational level of the parents, for not only will this affect what Bourdieu calls the 'cultural capital' available in the home, but it may also influence the values which parents have and the decisions they make regarding the importance of a good education for their children. For fathers (FATHER'S EDUCATION) and mothers (MOTHER'S EDUCATION), educational level is a dichotomous variable based on whether or not they completed their schooling at the minimum leaving age. Other variables and factors measuring possible class advantages/disadvantages associated with social background include the higher class of either grandfather (GRANDPARENTS' CLASS), a measure of overcrowding in the home based on persons per room while the children were growing up (OVERCROWDING), and a measure of lack of basic amenities in the home (HOME AMENITIES).

Also related to the SAD thesis are a number of variables and factors associated with the education of the child and the support it received from the parents. PRE-SCHOOL EDUCATION indicates whether or not children attended any pre-school or nursery education facility before the age of 5, and TYPE OF SCHOOL distinguishes those receiving a private education at 16 from those attending state schools. FATHER READ and MOTHER READ indicate the degree to which father and mother respectively read to the child at age 7(weekly, occasionally or hardly ever), and PARENTAL INTEREST is a measure of parental interest in the schooling of the child at age 11 based upon the school's assessment of the interest demonstrated by the father and mother plus evidence on whether they had made contact with the school during the previous twelve months. There is also a factor, PARENTAL ASPIRATIONS, expressing the degree to which parents had high aspirations for their child at age 11 (this is based on their wish that the child should remain at school beyond the minimum leaving age, together with their hope that it should go on to some form of further education). Finally, the sex of the child is measured by GENDER.

Taken together, these thirteen measures cover a large number of the material and cultural advantages/disadvantages which sociologists down the years have identified in an attempt to explain why class origins should be expected to influence educational and occupational success later in life. Not everything, of course, has been included—there are no measures of peer group pressure, nor of the quality of personal interaction with teachers, nor of the capacity to mobilise contacts and social networks. Nevertheless, a range of measures encompassing class of parents and grandparents, education of parents, indicators of household deprivation such as overcrowding and lack of amenities, private schooling, pre-schooling, early exposure to books in the home, parental interest in and support for education, and parental aspirations for their children would seem to offer a fair basis for testing most of the fundamental claims on which the SAD thesis rests.

We can begin an empirical evaluation of the meritocracy and SAD theses by considering why some working-class children succeed when others do not, and why some middle-class children fail when others maintain or enhance the position achieved by their parents.

Table 6 (p. 60) gives the results of a 'logistic regression model' in which 4 meritocracy variables and 12 SAD variables are used to predict whether individuals born to class IV/V parents will remain where they are or move all the way up to class I/II. It demonstrates clearly that it is meritocratic variables—ability, motivation and attitudes to employment—which are the key factors distinguishing successful lower working-class children from those they leave behind them.

With 183 of these individuals ending up in class IV/V as compared with 258 ending up in class I/II, the best initial prediction that we can make of any individual's class destination is that he or she makes it to class I/II. Such a prediction will be accurate in 59 per cent of cases (see the first line in the 'per cent CORRECT' column of Table 6). What we now try to do is to improve this predictive accuracy by taking account of additional informa-tion. The model tells us that the single most important piece of information which we need to take into account is the ability test score achieved by these individuals when they were 11 years old. When these test scores are entered into our model ('step 1'), the accuracy of the predictions we can make rises sharply from 59 per cent correct to 70 per cent correct. We can improve this still further ('step 2') by taking account of the level of motivation at school when aged 16, for we see that this information improves our predictive powers by a further 3 per cent. One of the two remaining meritocracy indicators (work attitudes in adult life) plus just two of the SAD indicators (gender—women perform rather better than men; and grandfathers' class—those with grandfathers above class IV/V perform better) also have effects significant enough for them to be included in the final model, but together they only raise the level of predictive accuracy by a further 3 percentage points.

In addition to telling us about how powerfully we can predict any individual's final class position, the model in Table 6 also tells us the relative contribution made by each factor in influencing this outcome. This is expressed by the final 'partial correlation coefficients' ('FINAL R') which indicate the relative effect of each variable in the model when the effects of all other variables are taken into account. From Table 6 it is clear that ability (R=0.26) is by far the strongest influence on working-class success, with motivation (R=0.16) and attitudes to work (R=0.15) as contributory factors.

The final column in the table ('FINAL EXP B') tells us, for each of the variables in the model, the factor by which the odds of entering class I/II change for each unit increase in the variable in question. For example, the odds of a class IV/V child entering class I/II relative to the odds of remaining in class IV/V are 258/183=1:1.4. These odds are improved by (1.4 x 1.06) for each point scored on the ability test, by (1.4 x 0.9) for each point on the motivation scale,[2] by (1.4 x 2.05) if the individual is female, and so on.

Perhaps the most striking feature of Table 6 (p. 60) concerns the list of variables which fail to enter the model. Some, like private schooling, are hardly surprising, for very few of these children attended fee-paying schools. Others, however, are surprising from the perspective of the SAD hypothesis. Material deprivation in the home (measured by overcrowding and by lack of basic amenities) has no significant effect. Nor do parental levels of education, exposure to books at an early age, pre-school play group or nursery attendance, parental interest in the child's schooling, or parental aspirations for the child's future. To the extent that we can predict success for children from classes IV and V, the key factors have to do with their ability and their attitudes to work (at school and in later employment) and have very little or nothing to do with material conditions or 'cultural capital' in the home.

We saw in chapter 4 that ability tests such as the one utilised in the NCDS are often criticised as in some way class-biased. In Table 6 (and in Table 7 p. 61), however, all children come from the same class background, so this sort of criticism cannot apply in these cases. The test which all these children took at age 11 is a good predictor of eventual occupational destination even when the children being compared come from comparable backgrounds. Clearly, the test results do indicate differences in individual aptitudes which cannot be explained away as merely the effects of social class background.

Table 7 outlines a similar logistic regression model, this time predicting failure (i.e. downward mobility out of class I/II) of middle-class children. Again, the basic message is the same—ability is the key factor with an R (0.19) twice as strong as that of any other variable in the model, and motivation is entered second. Private schooling appears as the most important of the SAD indicators, suggesting that the private schools may (as is often argued) offer middle-class parents some means of insuring their less able offspring against downward mobility. Parental education levels, absenteeism at school, attitudes to work and gender (where this time males prove rather more successful than females) all achieve statistical significance but make only tiny contributions to the final model.

Clearly, the meritocratic thesis proves much stronger than the SAD thesis in explaining why some individuals succeed while others from comparable social backgrounds do not. The meritocracy thesis has, however, to be subjected to a much stronger test. Supporters of the SAD thesis may well be willing to accept that individual qualities can make *some* difference to where people end up in life—that dull and lazy middle-class children are more likely to fail than bright and hard-working ones, or that intelligent and motivated working-class children are more likely to succeed than their less intelligent and less committed peers. The key question, however, is whether such individual qualities outweigh the initial advantages or disadvantages experienced by children growing up in *different* social environments. For example, are dull middle-class children still likely to do better than bright children from class IV/V backgrounds?

The short answer to this is that they are not. Class I/II children who retained their middle-class position had achieved an average score of 54.2 on the general ability test as compared with 46.2 for those who fell to class III and 41.5 for those falling to class IV/V. Class IV/V children who achieved entry to class I/II had an average score of 47.2 as compared with 39.0 for those entering class III and just 33.0 for those who stayed in class IV/V. These are statistically highly significant differences ($F=131.0$ with 5 df). Not only do ability scores within each class of origin sharply distinguish those who later succeed from those who do not, but class IV/V children entering the middle-class have significantly higher average ability scores than class I/II children leaving it.

Given that the IQ test sat by these children may well have favoured those from middle-class homes, this is a particularly striking result. Despite the cultural advantages which might have been expected to inflate their test scores, the middle-class failures scored lower on average than the successful children from the least advantaged semi-skilled and unskilled manual worker backgrounds. The 'real' difference in average levels of intelligence between them was almost certainly greater than the difference recorded in their test scores, given the likelihood that the middle-class children over-achieved on this test while the lower working-class children under-achieved. Clearly, the occupational system has sorted them out by intelligence to a much greater extent than it has selected them according to their class origins.

In order to evaluate the relative importance of ability and effort on the one hand, and social advantages and disadvantages on the other, we can develop what is called a 'multiple regression model' which includes all the meritocracy and SAD variables and factors and sorts them out in terms of the relative contribution which each of them makes to individuals' final destinations. To do this, we take as the measure of occupational success at 33 the ratings of their jobs on a 70-point occupational prestige scale.[3] All of the variables entered into the model are the same as in Tables 6 and 7 (pp. 60 and 61), and the results are summarised in Table 8 (p. 61).

In Table 8, the 'CHANGE IN R^2' column tells us how well the model is predicting occupational status at each step in its construction. For example, at step 1, we include ability test scores as the single most powerful predictor of people's occupational status at age 33, and these scores immediately explain 14 per cent of the variance in occupational statuses. At step 2, the next most powerful predictor, motivation, is added, and this raises the proportion of variance explained by the model to 16 per cent. And so on. The standardised Beta coefficients in the last column of the table (headed 'FINAL BETA') express the relative strength of each item in the model, after allowing for associations between the items. For example, with a coefficient of 0.25, the ability test scores have an effect on occupational status which is twice as strong as motivation (0.13), three times as strong as class background (0.8), and so on.

All four of the meritocracy variables enter the model, but, as before, ability is entered first and has by far the strongest effect (Beta=0.25) of any of the variables and factors in the model, while motivation at school enters second (Beta=0.13) and absenteeism at school and work attitudes enter fourth and sixth respectively, each with Betas=0.07. The strongest SAD variable in the model is parental class (Beta=0.08). Parental education levels, gender, parental interest in the child's schooling, private schooling and overcrowding in the home all achieve statistically significant effects, but they make only a tiny contribution to the overall model-fit. Grandparents' social class, pre-school education, early exposure to books and the level of basic amenities in the home all fail to achieve statistical significance. Basically, the model improves hardly at all after step 4—occupational status at age 33 is explained (to the extent that it is explained by any of these factors) mainly by ability, motivation, parental class and absenteeism, and of these four, ability appears roughly twice as important as motivation and three times more important than parental class and absenteeism.

It has also to be recognised, however, that the final model R-square (the total proportion of variance explained by the model) of 0.22 is fairly weak. The meritocracy thesis appears much stronger than the SAD thesis, but even when the two are combined, over three-quarters of the variance in occupational prestige scores remains unexplained. In part, this is because the model does not include direct measures of achievement which are obvious stepping stones to later occupational success. Three important measures are examination success at school, the occupational status of the first job taken after completing full-time education, and the achievement of further qualifications after leaving school. These three variables have been excluded until now because they are common to both the meritocracy and SAD theses. Both theories of social mobility accept that formal qualifications are important in influencing inter-generational mobility chances, and both accept that initial entry into the labour market is an important pointer to final class of destination. Where they differ is in the explanations they offer for why some people gain more qualifications than others, and why some enter the occupational system at a higher point than others.

Table 9 (p. 62) presents the results of a second multiple regression model entering the same variables and factors as before while adding school examination results summarised on a 9-point scale (EXAM PASSES AT 16), the occupational prestige of the first job after leaving school (CLASS FIRST JOB) and additional qualifications achieved after leaving school summarised on a 5-point scale (FURTHER QUALS). The model-fit is improved substantially (R-square=0.32) and all three variables are entered into the model before any of the meritocracy or SAD variables. With Beta values of 0.19 and 0.22 respectively, the model clearly demonstrates the importance for final occupational status of formal qualifications achieved through school examinations and through further study after leaving school. The status of first job plays an important but less powerful role in the model (the NCDS panel members have undergone substantial intragenerational as well as intergenerational mobility), and the only other variable which continues to have a relatively strong effect on class of destination is ability (Beta=0.13). This suggests that bright people tend to end up in higher status jobs, partly because they accumulate more qualifications, but also because their ability comes to be recognised and rewarded independently of their paper qualifications.[4] All three motivational factors are also included in this final model, as are parental class and overcrowding (which is probably an indicator of childhood poverty), but all make only tiny contributions with standardised coefficients of 0.06 or below.

How are we to summarise the evidence presented in this chapter? The evidence has been presented in three parts. First, we have seen that ability correlates more strongly with class of destination than with class of origin. Middle-class children tend to score higher than working-class children on ability tests (and on more specific tests of literacy and numeracy), but this is consistent with both the meritocracy and SAD hypotheses and in itself does not therefore tell us a great deal. What is more interesting is the relatively higher correlation between ability test scores and the class of destination achieved over twenty years after the test was taken, for this shows that the occupational class system is to some extent selecting by ability irrespective of social class origins. This finding is consistent with the meritocracy thesis but is inconsistent with the SAD thesis.

Second, we have also seen that ability and motivation are the key predictors of lower working-class success and of middle-class failure. Low ability does not necessarily prevent entry into the middle-class (not even for children from lower class backgrounds), and this suggests that other personal characteristics—a willingness to take risks, perhaps, or an engaging personality—may provide other routes to occupational success. High ability does, however, tend to safeguard individuals against failure, for very few high ability people ended up in classes IV and V irrespective of where they started out from. Bright and committed children tend to end up in the middle-class irrespective of whether they began life there or started out with class IV/V parents, although the former still enjoy a higher chance of success than the latter. Social mobility disparity ratios comparing class I/II origins with class IV/V origins are roughly halved once ability differentials between the classes are taken into account.

Third, we have seen that class destinations reflect individual merit (ability and motivation) much more than class background. Many of the factors which have attracted so much academic attention from sociologists down the years—private schooling, parental contact with schools, material conditions in the home, the 'cultural capital' passed on by middle-class parents to their children, and even gender bias in the school or the workplace—turn out, even when statistically significant, to exert only relatively minor effects on people's class destinies. By contrast, the factors which sociologists have so often ignored, or even dismissed as self-evidently absurd or unimportant—factors having to do with the intellectual capacities of individuals and the tenacity they display in working towards a given objective—turn out to be much more important.

None of this is sufficient to justify the claim that occupational class recruitment in Britain is entirely based on meritocratic principles. The high degree of variance left unexplained by the various models indicates that there are other factors at work which have little to do with either social advantage/disadvantage or meritocracy, and the models also suggest that both of the theses we have considered have something to offer to an overall explanation of class destinations. Nevertheless, the evidence does conclusively demonstrate that the occupational class system in Britain is more meritocratic than has commonly been assumed, and that initial patterns of social advantage or disadvantage are much less significant than has generally been claimed. In a straight evaluation of the meritocratic and SAD theses as explanations of social mobility and class recruitment, the former receives much more empirical support than the latter.

Table 2
Intergenerational Social Mobility Rates Based on Father's Class
(higher class of either father or mother in brackets)

(a) Percentage from Different Class Origins Arriving at each Class Destination (read across):

		Child's Class Age 33		
		I/II	III	IV/V
Class Origin				
	I/II	63(59)	31(33)	7(8)
	III	37(37)	49(49)	14(15)
	IV/V	28(27)	49(51)	23(22)

(b) Percentage in Each Class from Different Class Origins (read down):

		Child's Class Age 33		
		I/II	III	IV/V
Class Origin				
	I/II	42(46)	20(25)	14(21)
	III	46(44)	60(57)	56(55)
	IV/V	12(10)	20(17)	30(24)

Table 3
Social mobility disparity ratios (NCDS data)

	Relative Chances of being in:	
	Class I/II	Class IV/V
Father Class I/II	2.21	set at 1
Father Class III	1.29	2.18
Father Class IV/V	set at 1	3.47

Table 4
Mean ability scores by class of origin (higher parental class) and class of destination

Class of Origin	Mean Test Score	Std Deviation	Class of Destination	Mean Test Score	Std Deviation
I/II	50.6	14.3	I/II	51.6	13.7
III	44.0	15.0	III	42.2	14.7
IV/V	40.2	15.3	IV/V	36.3	14.8

r=0.24 (N=5565, missing=1230)   r=0.37 (N=5826, missing=969)

(Mean test score for total sample=45.4 on 80 items, standard deviation=14.3)

Table 5

**Social Mobility Disparity Ratios Above
and Below Threshold Ability Score for Class I/II Entry
*(whole sample in brackets)***

(a) Those scoring high enough for class I / II entry:

	Relative Chances of being in:	
	Class I/II	Class IV/V
Father Class I/II	1.67(2.21)	set at 1
Father Class III	1.23(1.29)	1.71(2.18)
Father Class IV/V	set at 1	3.50(3.47)

(b) Those scoring below threshold entry for class I / II

	Relative Chances of being in:	
	Class I/II	Class IV/V
Father Class I/II	2.13(2.21)	set at 1
Father Class III	1.15(1.29)	1.72(2.18)
Father Class IV/V	set at 1	2.31(3.47)

Table 6

**A Logistic Regression Model Predicting Class IV/V Children Entering
Class I/II Against Those Remaining in Class IV/V**

STEP	VARIABLE	% CORRECT	FINAL R	FINAL EXP (B)
0		58.5		
1	ABILITY TEST SCORE	69.6	0.26	1.06
2	MOTIVATION	73.0	0.16	0.90
3	WORK ATTITUDES	74.1	0.15	1.59
4	GENDER (FEMALE)	75.7	0.10	2.05
5	GRANDPARENTS' CLASS	76.0	0.09	0.63

Variables not in the equation: MOTHER READ, FATHER READ, MOTHER EDUCATION, FATHER EDUCATION, PRE-SCHOOL EDUCATION, TYPE OF SCHOOL, HOME AMENITIES, OVERCROWDING, PARENTAL ASPIRATIONS, PARENTAL INTEREST, ABSENTEEISM.

N=441

Table 7
A Logistic Regression Model Predicting Class I/II Children Entering Class I/II Against Those Who are Downwardly Mobile

STEP	VARIABLE	% CORRECT	FINAL R	FINAL EXP (B)
0		60.0		
1	ABILITY TEST SCORE	66.1	0.19	1.04
2	MOTIVATION	66.6	0.10	0.94
3	TYPE OF SCHOOL	67.5	0.07	1.92
4	MOTHER'S EDUCATION	67.7	0.05	1.36
5	ABSENTEEISM	68.1	0.04	0.79
6	FATHER'S EDUCATION	68.1	0.04	1.34
7	WORK ATTITUDES	68.9	0.04	1.15
8	GENDER (MALE)	68.7	0.04	0.76

Variables not in the equation: MOTHER READ, FATHER READ, PRE-SCHOOL EDUCATION, GRANDPARENTS' CLASS, HOME AMENITIES, OVERCROWDING, PARENTAL ASPIRATIONS, PARENTAL INTEREST.

N=1830

Table 8
A Multiple Regression model with Hope-Goldthorpe rank scores as dependent variable[5]

STEP	VARIABLE	CHANGE IN R^2	FINAL BETA
1	ABILITY TEST SCORE	0.14	0.25
2	MOTIVATION	0.16	0.13
3	PARENTAL CLASS	0.18	0.08
4	ABSENTEEISM	0.19	0.07
5	MOTHERS EDUCATION	0.20	0.06
6	WORK ATTITUDES	0.20	0.07
7	GENDER (MALE)	0.21	0.07
8	FATHERS EDUCATION	0.21	0.05
9	PARENTAL INTEREST	0.22	0.05
10	TYPE OF SCHOOL	0.22	0.05
11	OVERCROWDING	0.22	0.03

Variables not in the equation: FATHER READ, MOTHER READ, PRE-SCHOOL EDUCATION, GRANDPARENTS' CLASS, HOME AMENITIES.

Tests for multicollinearity: no variables correlated at higher than 0.5. Lowest tolerance (0.68) and highest Variance Inflation Factor (1.46) on ABILITY TEST SCORE. Inspection of variance proportions on eigenvalues shows some dependency between MOTHER'S EDUCATION (59%) and FATHER'S EDUCATION (63 %), and between ABILITY TEST SCORE (60%) and MOTIVATION (35%).

Table 9

**A Multiple Regression model including qualifications
and status of first job as independent variables**

STEP	VARIABLE	CHANGE IN R^2	FINAL BETA
1	EXAM PASSES AT 16	0.23	0.19
2	FURTHER QUALS	0.28	0.22
3	CLASS FIRST JOB	0.30	0.13
4	ABILITY TEST SCORE	0.31	0.13
5	PARENTAL CLASS	0.31	0.06
6	ABSENTEEISM	0.32	0.04
7	GENDER (MALE)	0.32	0.05
8	MOTIVATION	0.32	0.05
9	WORK ATTITUDES	0.32	0.04
10	OVERCROWDING	0.32	0.03

Variables not in the equation: MOTHERS EDUCATION, FATHERS EDUCATION, MOTHER READ, FATHER READ, PRESCHOOL EDUCATION, TYPE OF SCHOOL, GRANDPARENTS CLASS, HOME AMENITIES, PARENTAL INTEREST.

Tests for multicollinearity: no variables correlated at higher than 0.5 except EXAM PASSES AT 16 with ABILITY TEST SCORE (0.54) and EXAM PASSES AT 16 with FURTHER QUALS (0.54).

Pathways to Success

MANY different factors influence our occupational class destinies. Two of the most important are our mental ability and our motivation to succeed, but other things also play a part. Looking back over Tables 6 to 9, we see that social background and social identities can have an influence, albeit a lesser one. If you are born to semi- or unskilled working-class parents (Table 6 p. 60), you are much more likely to succeed in life if you are bright and hard working, but it also seems to help a little if you are female and if your grandparents were from a higher social class. If you are born to middle-class parents (Table 7 p. 61), you are much more likely to follow in your parents' footsteps if you are bright and hard working, but it can also help if you are sent to a private school, if your parents were well educated, and if you are male. Taking the picture overall (Tables 8 and 9 pp. 61 and 62), qualifications, ability and motivation stand out as the key factors predicting where we end up in the occupational hierarchy, but our parents (their social class, their level of education, and their degree of interest in our schooling), our gender (males tend to do a bit better), the type of school we attend (a private education helps), and conditions in the home (overcrowding hinders success) all seem to count for something.

Occupational recruitment, therefore, is largely meritocratic, but not wholly so. Social background does still play some part, and the fact that we have succeeded in explaining no more than one-third of the variance indicates that other factors are also involved which we have not succeeded in identifying or measuring and which probably have little to do with either merit or social background. The importance of sheer luck should not be overlooked.

The picture, therefore, is a complicated one. We can try to clarify it by tracing the patterns of causation and influence between all these different factors. To do this, we construct what is called a 'path model' (Figure 5, adjacent to back cover)[1] where occupational prestige at age 33 (the 'Hope-Goldthorpe' scale) is the dependent variable to be explained. For these purposes we concentrate solely on the 4,298 men who are in full-time employment at age 33 and on whom NCDS provides adequate information (the equivalent path model for women is, in fact, very little different).

How has this model been constructed? We began with some seventy variables taken from the NCDS data and measured at different time periods corresponding to the different 'sweeps' of the survey. These are organised sequentially—as we look from left to right of Figure 5, we move from indicators measured in 1958, when the children were born, through indicators measured at ages 7, 11 and 16, to those measured in 1991, when the panel members were aged 33. Indicators in boxes are *variables* which were directly measured in the survey (father's education, for example, is based on a question which asked the age at which panel members' fathers completed their full-time education). Indicators in circles are derived *factors* based on a weighted combination of variables from the survey which are closely associated with one another (academic ability at age 7, for example, is derived from the scores on both the English and maths tests which children took in 1965; academic ability at 11 is based on the English and maths scores in 1969 as well as the scores on the general ability test taken at that time; and so on). A factor can be understood as a 'latent' variable in that it refers to some 'hidden' phenomenon which cannot be directly measured (in this example, academic ability) but which is assumed to be the common cause of the high degree of co-variation between some cluster of observed variables (in this example, maths test scores, English test scores, etc.).

The straight line arrows running between the different variables and factors in the diagram indicate a causal influence (curved double-headed arrows indicate correlation without imputed causation), and the coefficients on each arrow are the standardised (Beta) weights (similar to the Beta coefficients in the multiple regression models outlined in Tables 8 and 9 (pp. 61 and 62) which enable us to gauge the relative impact of the different causal connections. For example, there are four straight line arrows running from academic ability at age 7. The strongest (r=0.71) runs to academic ability at age 11 (this tells us that scores on the English and maths tests taken at age 7 are very strongly predictive of scores on the English, maths and general ability tests taken four years later). Other effects are somewhat weaker but are still quite powerful: the child's ability at 7 influences the child's aspirations at 11 (r=0.30), the parents' aspirations for the child at age 11 (r=0.27), and the parents' lack of interest in the child's education at 11 (the negative coefficient of -0.24 indicating that high ability scores produce low levels of 'lack of interest'—in other words, high interest).

In generating a model like this, we are looking to achieve two things. First, the model must 'fit' the data. Obviously, a perfect fit could be achieved by drawing arrows between every variable and factor, for this will pick up all the effects of all the variables we are looking at. This, however, would be pointless, for our aim is to come up with the simplest model we can find. The second thing we are hoping to achieve, therefore, is to end up with a parsimonious model—one which contains the smallest number of variables, and the smallest number of arrows, while still achieving an acceptable level of fit with the data. As we develop the model, clustering variables into factors, and removing arrows between variables and factors, so the model becomes simpler (our second aim), but model-fit deteriorates (taking us away from our first aim). Finding the balance between degree of fit and overall simplicity is like walking a tightrope. We remove an arrow and the model wobbles horribly as the statistics measuring model-fit plummet; we reinstate the arrow, remove a different one, and find that the model-fit is hardly affected at all. And so we proceed, until eventually we end up with a model which fits the data well and which cannot be further simplified without producing a significant deterioration in degree of fit. This is the model represented in Figure 5 (adjacent to back cover).[2]

Absence of variables in Figure 5 indicates that they had virtually no influence on any of the other variables in the model and could therefore be removed. This was true, for example, of pre-school education (which seems to have had no significant effect), and of parents who read to the children at 7 as compared with those who did not. Similarly, absence of an arrow between any two variables or factors indicates that there is no significant direct effect linking one to the other, or that the effect was so weak that it could be excluded without seriously weakening overall model-fit. Attendance at private school at the age of 7, for example, reduces parental lack of interest in the child's education at age 11 (r=-0.8), but there is no arrow to the child's aspirations at age 11 indicating that private schooling at 7 had little or no impact on children's aspirations four years later.

The fact that there is no direct effect (i.e. no arrow) between two variables or factors does not necessarily mean that the first is having no significant influence on the second, for its effect may be indirect via some third variable or factor in the model. Private schooling at 7, for example, has no *direct* effect on the child's aspirations at 11 (for there is no arrow linking them), but we can trace an *indirect* effect via parental lack of interest in the child's education (i.e. arrows link private schooling to parental interest, and parental interest to the child's aspirations). This suggests that private schooling at 7 increases the level of parental interest at 11 which in turn raises the child's aspirations.

To calculate the strength of indirect effects of one variable on another, we multiply the coefficients along the arrows which link them (in this example, -0.08 x -0.19, which gives an effect of private schooling on children's aspirations of 0.015). It is therefore possible, by tracing the different pathways through the model, to calculate for any given variable both the direct effects and the indirect effects which it has on the final outcome (occupational prestige at age 33), and if we sum the direct and indirect effects, we can find the total effect of each variable or factor. This has been done in Table 10 (p. 73).[3]

Before considering Table 10, it is worth inspecting the path diagram visually. We see that there are only four arrows pointing to occupational prestige at age 33. The two strongest come from qualifications achieved after leaving school (r=0.25) and from ability as measured at age 11 (r=0.25). These direct effects are twice as strong as academic qualifications achieved at school (r=0.13) and motivation at school at age 16 (r=-0.13).[4] There is no direct effect from any of the social background variables. This confirms the results of the previous chapter—the strong direct influences on class destination are those which have to do with the individual's ability, motivation and qualifications.

As we move backwards through the diagram, however, we see that other factors are having some indirect effect. To some extent, of course, taking account of indirect effects further strengthens the initial conclusion that individual ability is a crucial influence, for not only does ability at 11 directly affect class at 33 (r=0.25), but it also has numerous indirect effects which also have to be added in. For example, the path from ability at 11 via qualifications at 16 to class at 33 shows an additional (indirect) effect of ability at 11 of 0.34 x 0.13 = 0.044; the path from ability at 16 via qualifications at 16 to class at 33 shows an additional indirect effect of 0.11 x 0.13 = 0.014; and so on. But taking account of indirect effects also reveals the way in which social background is influencing class destination. For example, father's class has no direct effect, but there are many indirect effects. Fathers class when the child was 11, for example, influences the child's motivation at 16 (r=0.21) which in turn influences class at 33 (r=0.13)—an indirect effect of 0.028. Similarly, there are pathways from father's class at 11, through parental interest in child's schooling at 16 (r=0.17), child's aspirations at 16 (-0.14), and qualifications at 16 (r=0.37) to class at 33 (r=0.13)—an indirect effect of 0.0011—and from father's class at 7 through crowded accommodation at 11 (-0.14) and at 16 (0.43) to motivation at 16 (r=0.06), and from there to class at 33 (r=-0.13)—an indirect effect of 0.00047.

Once we begin tracing long and complex paths of indirect causation, the diagram swiftly becomes virtually unintelligible, and at this point we need to turn to the summary statistics in Table 10 (p. 73). This table organises the variables and factors in the path diagram into three main categories—social advantages and disadvantages (parents' social class, parents' level of education, housing conditions and private schooling), parental behaviour and attitudes (parents' aspirations for the child and parents' interest in the child's schooling), and the individual's own characteristics and achievements (ability, ambition and qualifications achieved). For each variable or factor in each of these categories, the table gives the standardised direct effect on class at 33 together with the summed indirect effects along all the possible pathways, and in the final column, the total effect represents the sum of these two.

The column giving direct effects simply tells us what we already know from the path diagram—only four variables or factors feed directly into the occupational class achieved at 33, and these are all to do with the individual's own ability, motivation and qualifications. The second column shows that virtually all the variables and factors in the model nevertheless achieve some indirect effect on where people end up. The final column, however, simply confirms that when we look at total effects, taking account of all these indirect as well as direct effects, it is still an individual's characteristics which far outweigh the impact of social background and parental influence. For example, the influence of father's class throughout the period when the child is growing up works out at a combined standardised coefficient of $(0.12 + 0.18 + 0.03 + 0.03) = 0.36$, and the impact of parents' education (father and mother combined) is half as strong again (0.18). Parental aspirations throughout the period of childhood work out at a total coefficient of 0.17, and parental interest in the child's education (a factor derived from information about parents' school visits and teacher assessments of the level of parental interest) comes out at a total of 0.30. All of these factors are clearly important, but they are eclipsed by the combined effects of the two meritocracy factors. Thus the total effect of ability works out at 0.85, and that of childhood ambition and effort comes out at 0.55. Summarising all of this, we may say that, in predicting where people are likely to end up in the class system at age 33, their ability alone is well over twice as important as their class origins, three times more powerful than the degree of interest their parents showed in their schooling, and is five times more powerful than their parents' level of education or the aspirations which their parents harboured for them while they were growing up.

Of course, critics of the meritocracy thesis might still reasonably point out that social background is still having a sizeable effect. Class origins, in particular, do seem to have a marked impact on people's class destinations, even if it is only half as great as the effect of their ability. Table 11 (p. 74) enables us to address this point by tracing the pathways through which social background factors make themselves felt. In this table, the total standardised effects of each factor or variable are broken down by the route it follows in influencing class at 33. The first column identifies the amount of the effect which is transmitted via the individual's ability. The second identifies the effect routed via the individual's ambition. The third identifies the effect which is exerted through neither ability nor ambition.

We see immediately that virtually everything that has an influence on people's class destinations does so by virtue of its association with either ability or motivation. If we consider father's class, for example, we find that roughly half of its overall effect on where children end up is mediated by the child's ability, and half by the child's ambition, and that there is no effect other than via these two.

This is a fascinating and important result. We already know (from the lack of any direct effect from father's class to child's class at 33) that the influence of people's class origins on their class destinations has nothing to do with things like accent, 'linguistic codes', teacher bias, or special contacts which they may have, for if these sorts of factors (which were not included in the model) were important, there would be a direct line in the path diagram from father's class to class of destination by-passing all the other variables which were included in the model. There is no such line, and this indicates that the full effects of class background have been captured by the variables included in the model.

The additional information that class origins only operate within the model via the ability and the ambition of the child also now tells us *how* class background has the effect that it does. It is because middle-class parents have children of higher academic ability and children who are more motivated and hard working at school. Ability and ambition are not simply, or even mainly, a function of class background (it is quite possible for working-class children to be bright and ambitious), but the effect that class background does have is almost entirely a function of its association with the different average levels of ability and ambition of children from different social classes.

Why are children from higher social classes more ambitious? The answer can be found elsewhere in Table 11 (p. 74). If we look at parental aspirations, we see that high aspirations by parents (measured by a desire for children to stay on at school and/or to pursue further or higher education) have an impact on class at 33 mainly through their effects on children's own ambitions and motivations (0.17), but that high aspirations have virtually no effect through raising children's ability as measured by test performances at 7, 11, and 16. Ambitious parents raise motivated children, but they probably do not raise brighter children (this is confirmed in Figure 5 [adjacent to back cover] by the absence of any direct arrows linking parental aspiration factors to ability factors). And parental aspirations are in turn linked to the social class of parents (mainly through the direct arrow in Figure 5 from father's class in 1965 to parental aspirations in 1969).

Why do middle-class parents raise more able children? This is a more difficult question to answer. We have already discussed it at length in earlier chapters where we saw that the answer almost certainly lies in some combination of nature and nurture. Middle-class parents are themselves likely to be more intelligent (which is part of the reason that they got into the middle-class in the first place), and will therefore pass on some of their intellectual advantages to their offspring. They will also, however, provide an environment which fosters the intellectual ability of their children.

Figure 5 and Table 11 help us unpack this in a little more detail. Ability is a remarkably constant factor over time—the standardised coefficient linking ability at 7 to ability at 11 is very high at 0.71. Amazingly, the results of the very brief tests (ten sums for maths and a simple word recognition test for English) which these children did at age 7 provide a powerful predictor of their maths, English and general ability (IQ) scores at 11, which in turn strongly influence their later educational and occupational careers.

From Figure 5 we see that there are four arrows leading directly to ability at 7. Two of these, from father's education and mother's education, are fairly weak (0.09 and 0.11 respectively), yet it is precisely the educational level of the parents which we should expect to have the most powerful effects on ability were 'nurture' to be the key factor in shaping intelligence, for better educated parents will presumably provide an environment more conducive to learning. The other two arrows are stronger—a coefficient of -0.23 links father's class at 7 to child's ability at 7,[5] and a coefficient of 0.29 links parental interest in education at 7 to child's ability at 7—though there is no very strong predictor of child's ability anywhere in the model. Parental lack of interest in education is itself directly linked to the father's class (r=0.30) but it has a sizeable effect on the child's ability over and above this. What all this means is that middle-class parents tend to have bright children, but so too do parents who are interested in their children's schooling, irrespective of which class they belong to.

There are at least three plausible explanations for the effects of parental interest in education on children's measured ability. One is that parents who are supportive of their children's education thereby raise the ability of their children (i.e. a supportive home environment raises IQ). This seems the most obvious interpretation, and it is, of course, consistent with the argument of those who believe that IQ is simply a function of environment rather than of innate ability. It is, however, difficult to square this interpretation with the evidence that parents who are ambitious for their children have little success in raising their children's IQ scores. It is also inconsistent with the evidence that parents who read to their children, or who organise pre-school education for their children, thereby achieve no significant impact on their children's measured ability.

How else might this association be explained? A second possible explanation is that parents who realise early on that they have a bright child then become interested in his or her education (i.e. a high IQ child stimulates interest in the parents which would not otherwise be there). This seems plausible, as does a third interpretation—that intelligent parents of whatever class and education level are more likely (a) to realise the importance of education for their children (and are therefore more interested), and (b) to produce children who are also intelligent like themselves (i.e. parental interest in education is simply an indirect indicator of parental intelligence). In the end, we cannot judge from the data which of these explanations is the most likely—the data are consistent with both 'nature' and 'nurture' hypotheses—but we clearly should not jump to the most obvious as being the most likely.

The other interesting point to pick out of Table 11 relates to the effects of private schooling. Judged by the size of the standardised coefficients, these effects are very small (a conclusion which is consistent with the findings of the multiple regression models in chapter 7), but it is interesting that private secondary schooling is one of only two variables in the entire model which has an effect on class destinations which is not routed entirely through pathways connected with either ability or ambition. Figure 5 demonstrates that private schooling affects motivation at 16 (r=0.11) and children's aspirations at 16 (r=0.12)—it does, in other words, seems to make children more ambitious and hard working—and there is also a small effect on ability at 16 (r=0.07), which suggests that private schooling improves maths and English capabilities to some extent. But there is also a fourth arrow leading directly to qualifications at 16. Again, the standardised coefficient is small (r=0.07), but it is statistically significant, and its removal would adversely effect the degree of fit of the model. This indicates that private schools tend to do better than state schools at getting children through examinations, irrespective of their abilities or their ambition.

Does this represent an important dent in the meritocracy hypothesis? On the face of it, not really, for the size of the coefficients is tiny, and from Table 10 (p. 73) we see that the total contribution of private secondary schooling to occupational success at 33 amounts to just 0.02 (about one-fortieth of the total effect attributable to ability). We need to be cautious, however, for we are dealing all the time here with *standardised* coefficients. In most cases, this is not a problem—standardisation is enormously helpful in enabling us to gauge the relative strength of effects of different variables in the model, for the variables are all measured on different scales and standardisation renders them comparable on a single scale. In the case of private schooling, however, it may be a problem, for only a very small proportion of the children in the sample went to private schools. This means that, for private schooling to have a strong effect as a predictor within the model as a whole, it would have to have a huge effect at the level of each individual attending a private school. The tiny standardised coefficients tell us only that in Britain, private schooling is relatively unimportant (as compared with other factors like ability, parental class, or ambition) in helping us explain the pattern of class recruitment, but this may simply reflect the fact that so very few people actually attend private schools that its overall effect is massively diluted.

One way in which we might check to see whether private schooling has an important impact on class destinations for those (relatively few) individuals who receive it is to examine the raw coefficients before they are standardised. The raw coefficients tell us the effect of a one unit change in the values of the variables we are looking at. Private schooling at age 16, for example, is a variable with just two values (either people did attend or did not attend a private school), and it has a total (unstandardised) effect on occupational prestige of 0.14. Father's class, by contrast, is a variable with three values (middle-class, intermediate class, lower working-class). Father's class in 1965 (when the children were aged 7) has a total (unstandardised) effect of 0.28, which means that there is a 0.28 size effect for each value of father's class (i.e. a 0.56 effect when comparing middle-class with lower working-class). When we consider only the standardised total effects of private schooling at 16 and father's class at 7 (Table 10), it seems that the latter variable is nine times more powerful than the former (their standardised coefficients are 0.18 and 0.02 respectively). Looking at the raw coefficients, however, shows that, even when we take the extreme values (middle-class versus lower working-class), the impact of father's class on occupational prestige at 33 is in fact only four times stronger than the effect of private schooling (0.56 against 0.14). It does seem from this that the use of standardised coefficients is artificially deflating the importance of private schooling for those who receive it.

Unfortunately, our use of raw coefficients is limited by the fact that they are virtually meaningless when calculated for the latent factors in the model (i.e. all those indicators which were derived from clusters of variables and which appear in circles in Figure 5 [adjacent to back cover]), for latent factors are constructs with no meaningful scale of values. This means that we cannot use raw coefficients to compare, say, the effect of private schooling with the effect of ability, or of parental aspirations. We might say that, relative to other directly measured variables (like father's class), the standardised coefficients for private schooling appear to under-
emphasise its total effect by a factor of two or more (i.e. private schooling is twice or three times more powerful than the standardised coefficients suggest), in which case we should perhaps double or treble its relative strength when comparing it with the latent factors in Table 10 (p. 73). Even if we make this adjustment, however, the impact of private schooling remains relatively small (an adjusted standardised coefficient of, say, 0.06).

Where does all this leave us? Table 12 (p. 75) summarises the proportion of the variance in occupational status at age 33 which is explained by the various factors and variables in the model, and this perhaps represents the simplest and most useful summary of the findings. The 'variance' of a variable can be understood as the average amount by which each case differs from the mean score of the total population. Our measure of occupational prestige at age 33 ranks different jobs, according a low score to those with low status, and a high score to those with a high one. If we calculate the variance of this variable, we can calculate the average amount by which the rankings of people's jobs are scattered over the whole range of this scale. Put another way, variance is a measure of the degree of spread or dispersal of cases on any given variable.

When we construct explanatory models such as the one outlined in Figure 5, we are essentially trying to explain this dispersal. In a sense, we assume that every individual would achieve the same occupational status score (i.e. the mean) were it not for the effects of particular variables and factors which cause them to score higher or lower. Thus, as we enter different explanatory factors and variables into the model, so the variance in occupational status decreases. The stronger the model, the higher the proportion of variance accounted for.

It can be seen from Table 12 that our model has accounted for around 35 per cent of the variance in occupational prestige scores at age 33. The key question is which of our explanatory factors and variables is achieving the greatest proportional increase in variance explained? The answer from the table is glaringly obvious—ability alone is accounting for half of it (17 per cent out of a total variance explained of 35 per cent). Nothing else comes close. Motivation accounts for 5 per cent, qualifications for 6 per cent, class origins for just 3 per cent. Of all the variables and factors we have been able to measure, ability is by far the most important, yet this is precisely the factor which the last fifty years of social mobility research in Britain has ignored!

This brings us to the end of two dense chapters in which we have exhaustively analysed a set of key variables using what is probably the best data set available to us in Britain. It has to be said that much remains unexplained by any of these variables—it is probably impossible ever to achieve a model which will come close to explaining most or all of the variance in where people end up in the occupational system, for in the end we are all unique individuals with our own unique personalities and biographies. Perhaps everything that happens in life has a cause, but in human societies, the causes are virtually infinite and the complexity of their interaction defies even the most sophisticated of modelling and measurement techniques. In constructing models such as those developed in the last two chapters, we are trying to render this bewildering complexity simple in order to make it amenable to generalisation. In the process, we inevitably lose sight of much of the uniqueness which makes every person different.

To the extent that we can generalise, however, we can conclude with some confidence that sociologists have for many years been barking up the wrong tree. If we are interested in identifying those factors which play the most important role in determining the social class positions which we all end up in, then we should be paying far more attention to factors to do with individuals themselves—especially their ability and their motivation—and we should be worrying much less than we have done about the effects of the social situations into which they are born and within which they grow up. It does make some difference whether your father is an unskilled manual worker or a well-paid professional, whether your mother left school at the minimum legal age or stayed on to do exams, whether your parents encouraged you in your school work or showed no interest in your education, whether they tried to motivate you with their ambitions for you or left you to find your own way, whether you attended a private school or a state comprehensive, whether you had your own bedroom in which to do your homework or had to share with a sibling—but in the end, what matters most is whether you are bright, and whether you work hard. This is precisely what the thesis of meritocracy is all about, and for this reason, the conclusion which surely now has to be drawn from the evidence we have reviewed is that Britain is, to a large extent, a meritocratic society which allocates people to occupational class positions mainly on the basis of ability plus effort.

Table 10
Summary of Standardised Direct, Indirect
and Total Effects in the Path Model

	DIRECT EFFECT	INDIRECT EFFECTS	TOTAL EFFECTS
(A) SOCIAL ADVANTAGES/DISADVANTAGES			
a.1: Parents Class and Education			
Grandparents' Class	-	0.05	0.05
Mother's Education Level	-	0.09	0.09
Father's Education Level	-	0.09	0.09
Father's Class in 1958	-	0.12	0.12
Father's Class in 1965 (additional effect)	-	0.18	0.18
Father's Class in 1969 (additional effect)	-	0.03	0.03
Father's Class in 1974 (additional effect)	-	0.03	0.03
Mother's Class in 1974	-	0.01	0.01
a.2: Housing Conditions			
Crowded accommodation at age 7	-	0.03	0.03
Crowded at age 11 (additional effect)	-	0.02	0.02
Crowded at age 16 (additional effect)	-	0.01	0.01
a.3: Schooling			
Private School age 7	-	0.01	0.01
Private School age 16 (additional effect)	-	0.02	0.02
(B) PARENTS BEHAVIOUR/ATTITUDES			
b.1: Aspirations for Child			
When Child aged 7	-	-	-
When aged 11 (additional effect)	-	0.04	0.04
When aged 16 (additional effect)	-	0.13	0.13
b.2: Interest in Child's Education			
When Child aged 7	-	0.14	0.14
When aged 11 (additional effect)	-	0.09	0.09
When aged 16 (additional effect)	-	0.07	0.07
(C) INDIVIDUAL CHARACTERISTICS			
c.1: Academic Ability			
Aged 7	-	0.39	0.39
Aged 11 (additional effect)	0.25	0.18	0.43
Aged 16 (additional effect)	-	0.03	0.03
c.2: Ambition			
Child's Aspirations aged 11	-	0.15	0.15
Child's Aspirations aged 16 (add. effect)	-	0.21	0.21
Motivation at School aged 16	0.13	0.06	0.19
c.3: Qualifications			
Qualifications at 16	0.13	0.10	0.23
Additional Qualifications by age 33	0.25	-	0.25

Table 11
Standardised Total Effects Operating Through
Ability, Ambition and Other Routes

	EFFECTS THROUGH ABILITY	EFFECTS THROUGH AMBITION	EFFECTS THROUGH NEITHER
(A) SOCIAL ADVANTAGES/DISADVANTAGES			
a.1: Parents Class			
Father's Class in 1958	0.09	0.06	-
Father's Class in 1965 (additional effect)	0.14	0.08	-
Father's Class in 1969 (additional effect)	-	0.03	-
Father's Class in 1974 (additional effect)	-	0.03	-
Mother's Class in 1974	-	0.01	-
a.2: Housing Conditions			
Crowded accommodation at age 7	0.02	0.02	-
Crowded at age 11 (additional effect)	0.01	0.01	-
Crowded at age 16 (additional effect)	-	0.01	-
a.3: Schooling			
Private School at age 7	0.02	-	-
Private School at age 16 (additional effect)	-	-	0.02
(B) PARENTS BEHAVIOUR/ATTITUDES			
b.1: Aspirations for Child			
When Child aged 7	-	-	-
When aged 11 (additional effect)	0.02	0.04	-
When aged 16 (additional effect)	0.01	0.13	-
b.2: Interest in Child's Education			
When Child aged 7	0.13	0.05	-
When aged 11 (additional effect)	0.07	0.05	-
When aged 16 (additional effect)	-	0.07	-
(C) INDIVIDUAL CHARACTERISTICS			
c.1: Academic Ability			
Aged 7	0.39	0.13	-
Aged 11 (additional effect)	0.18	0.09	-
Aged 16 (additional effect)	0.03	-	-
c.2: Ambition			
Child's Aspirations aged 11	0.08	0.15	-
Child's Aspirations aged 16 (add. effect)	0.01	0.21	-
Motivation at School aged 16	0.01	0.06	-
c.3: Qualifications			
Qualifications at 16	-	-	0.10
Additional Qualifications by age 33	-	-	-

Note: Total effects in Table 10 do not equal the summed effects (through ability, through ambition and through neither) in Table 11 for three reasons: (1) Table 10 'total effects' are total *net* effects along pathways containing both positive and negative coefficients; (2) some effects operate through *both* ability and ambition so the total effect cannot be derived by summing the effects through each pathway; and (3) figures have been rounded.

Table 12
Proportion of Variance in Occupational Prestige
Score at Age 33 Explained by Different Categories of Variables

CATEGORY	PROPORTION OF VARIANCE EXPLAINED
a1: Parents' Class	0.03
a2: Housing Condition	0.00*
a3: Schooling	0.00*
b1: Aspirations for Child	0.01
b2: Interest in Child's Education	0.03
c1: Academic Ability	0.17
c2: Ambition	0.05
c3: Qualifications	0.06
TOTAL VARIANCE EXPLAINED	0.35

* Less than 0.01

Do We Really *Want to Live in a Meritocratic Society?*

THE essence of a meritocratic society is that it offers individuals equal opportunities to become unequal. There is open competition for the most desirable, responsible and well-rewarded positions, and the most able and committed people generally succeed in attaining these positions.

It might be assumed that meritocracy is an ideal which is shared by virtually everybody. It seems to be a 'good thing', both for the society (for it ensures that the most talented people get into the key leadership positions) and for individuals themselves (for it respects and justly rewards individual achievement). Against this, however, a meritocracy can be an uncomfortable place in which to live, for it is inherently competitive, and it produces losers as well as winners. For this reason, the meritocracy ideal has many enemies, not least among egalitarians. In this final chapter, I shall therefore move beyond discussion of the evidence about whether Britain is meritocratic to consider the broader question of whether meritocracy as an ideal can be defended against its critics.

The meritocracy ideal is an individualistic ideal in that it celebrates individual achievement. The notion that individuals should be allocated to social positions on the basis of their talents and hard work, rather than according to their station at birth, is a relatively recent development with its origins in the development of political liberalism in Europe. Individualism did not originate in the modern period, for, especially in England, it has a long history,[1] but individualism lay at the heart of the modernist transition, and the belief in meritocracy is its legacy.

The fundamental sociological problem posed by the transition to modernity was how a mass society of autonomous individuals could be bonded together as a single, functioning unity. In modern societies governments are in principle answerable to the will of their citizens, rather than the masses being an instrument of the will of their leaders; duties and obligations arise out of voluntary legal contracts rather than from the sanctity of a traditional status order; individual conscience replaces the church as the final arbiter of morality; the pursuit of self-interest in the marketplace destroys the traditional authority and patronage of the landowning classes; and the blossoming of individual diversity is celebrated while the call to conformity is distrusted. But in such societies, where the individual is sovereign, what is there to hold us all together?

Emile Durkheim famously addressed (and largely answered) this question in his book, *The Division of Labour in Society*, first published over one hundred years ago.[2] Recognising that social life requires a moral foundation, Durkheim nevertheless argued that this did not mean that it was necessary to return to the repressive and homogenous 'collective conscience' which stifled individual diversity and enforced moral confor- mity in pre-modern times. Modern societies, he argued, were functionally differentiated as a result of an advanced social division of labour, and this was precisely the source of their strength. In modern societies, every individual is different, but no individual can be an island. Functional differentiation means that we all depend upon each other—together we thrive, divided we die. Like a complex living organism, modern society holds together by virtue of the complementary functions played by its many different parts, for there can be no stronger social adhesive than the fundamental need to co-operate with one's fellow human beings in order to survive and prosper.

Seen in this way, any attempt to impose a common morality in modern societies is not only doomed to fail, but it is in Durkheim's terms unneces- sary and fundamentally misguided. As Margaret Thatcher discovered when she advised a return to 'Victorian values', and as John Major found with his ill-fated and short-lived 'Back to Basics' campaign, the attempt to solve the moral problems of modern societies by appealing to the faded moral certainties of past ones is likely to produce widespread derision and resentment because it challenges the one moral value which we do all hold in common—the importance of tolerating and even encouraging individual diversity.[3] As Durkheim recognised, the only ethic which we all need to hold in common and which makes sense to modern individuals is one which emphasises and defends the right to be different.

But if the solution to the problem of social cohesion is not to be found in the imposition of common moralities, where is it to be found? Durkheim recognised that modern societies in his time were not generally harmoni- ous and well-functioning systems, and what was true at the end of the nineteenth century seems even more true today at the end of the twentieth. He was convinced, however, that modern social 'pathologies' were not the product of individual diversity. They were due, rather, to the fact that social organisation has failed to keep pace with other changes in society wrought by the transition to modernity.

As is well known, one of the pathologies which Durkheim identified was what he called *anomie*—the malady of infinite aspiration. In modern societies, individuals often fail to recognise the limits on what they can expect to get, and they lose sight of the norms governing the way they should go about getting it. Durkheim believed that this problem was in principle remediable, for what was required was new forms of social organisation based upon occupational communities which would reinforce our understanding of the bonds of interdependence which unite us.

What is perhaps less often remembered is that Durkheim then went on to identify a second problem in modern societies. This he referred to as the *forced division of labour*. For functional interdependence to produce social cohesion, it was imperative that the social division of labour be 'spontaneous' rather than coerced. Spontaneity here means that people should gravitate to the social positions for which they are naturally best suited. Individuals, he believed, would never be happy (and hence modern societies would never function properly) for as long as they were obliged to perform functions in the social division of labour which were inappropriate to their talents and potentials:

> For the division of labour to produce solidarity, it is not sufficient that each have his task; it is still necessary that this task be fitting to him ... If the institution of classes or castes sometimes gives rise to anxiety and pain instead of producing solidarity, this is because the distribution of social functions on which it rests does not respond, or rather no longer responds, to the distribution of natural talents ... The division of labour produces solidarity only if it is spontaneous and in proportion as it is spontaneous ... In short, *labour is divided spontaneously only if society is constituted in such a way that social inequalities exactly express natural inequalities*(emphasis added).[4]

Durkheim's argument here is crucial for our present purposes, for he is in effect arguing that social cohesion depends upon meritocracy. Individuals will not be happy, and modern societies will not function harmoniously, until natural inequalities are reflected in social inequalities. Were we to establish true equality of opportunity (and in Durkheim's view, this would mean abolishing the right to inherit property as well as extending access to education), individuals would distribute themselves between different social class positions in each generation on the basis of their natural talents, and there would no longer be any grounds for envy, bitterness or anger on the part of those at the bottom.

Durkheim's analysis represents a classic statement of the meritocracy ideal: class inequalities need not generate class antagonisms provided recruitment is open and the competition is fair, for it is in everybody's interest that the best people fill the top positions and that all individuals occupy the social roles to which they are naturally best suited.

This argument was subsequently further elaborated by sociologists in the USA in the 1950s who developed what they called a *functional theory of stratification*. Following Talcott Parsons, who saw that social stratification might contribute to social integration rather than tearing a society asunder, theorists like Kingsley Davis and Wilbert Moore proposed that societies need to recruit the most talented and able individuals to fill the most important positions, and that the only way of achieving this, short of physical coercion, is by means of some system of social inequality. They sought to demonstrate that the social positions of greatest functional importance (judged in terms of the number of other positions which depend upon them) tend in modern societies to be the most highly rewarded, and that a system of unequal financial rewards is necessary to encourage the most talented individuals to undergo the sacrifice of long-term training required by positions of high responsibility.[5] Like Durkheim, therefore, the functionalist theorists of the 1950s believed that social stratification could represent part of the solution to the problem of social cohesion, rather than (as in Marx's theory) part of the cause. For this to happen, however, it was necessary that talent be recognised and rewarded appropriately.

How plausible is all this? Is meritocracy consistent with, even necessary for, social cohesion in modern societies? There is an altogether opposite view which suggests that a meritocratic society will end up tearing itself apart.

Michael Young, the sociologist who first coined the term 'meritocracy' in the 1950s, provides a clear and provocative statement of this second position. In *The Rise of the Meritocracy*,[6] published in 1958, he developed a futuristic fable (a sort of 'social science fiction') purporting to be a social history of Britain written in the year 2034. His story tells of how an increasing premium had come to be placed on talent such that, by 1990, all individuals with high IQs were being recruited into the leading positions in society irrespective of their social backgrounds. This meant that the lower social strata were progressively stripped of their 'natural leaders' as talented individuals were selected out. Far from fostering social cohesion, as Durkheim would have predicted, this generated a festering resentment at the base of the society, for those individuals who remained in the lower strata were left to contemplate their own personal failure and could find nobody to blame but themselves. Residualised and marginalised by the stigma of failure, they were gradually attracted to a new form of radical populism aimed at replacing élitism based on intelligence with an egalitarian, classless society in which every individual was held in equal social esteem. Young's fable ends in the year 2033 when the Meritocracy was overthrown by a Populist revolt.

Young's thesis has recently been given credence from what might seem a very unlikely source. Richard Herrnstein and Charles Murray's *The Bell Curve* has, as we saw in chapter 5, attracted most attention for its claim that race and intelligence are related. The core thesis of the book, however, does not revolve around the issue of race. It is rather that meritocracy in the United States is generating a system of social stratification based upon 'cognitive classes', and that this threatens to undermine social cohesion.

Herrnstein and Murray base their analysis on two key propositions. First, class recruitment in the United States has become more open during the course of the twentieth century, and for the first time in its history, the most intelligent individuals are now being selected for élite membership irrespective of their social origins. The change has come about mainly through the expansion of higher education with college access now determined solely on the basis of ability. Secondly, the development of a high technology, knowledge-based society has meant that the number of jobs requiring high levels of intelligence and training has expanded, and that the market value of high intelligence has been rising. This means that the talented individuals from different social origins who get recruited into the 'cognitive élite' have been growing increasingly affluent.

As the brightest individuals are sucked out of the lower social strata, they come to form a relatively exclusive stratum based on membership of about a dozen main professions plus senior business executive positions. These people interact professionally and socially more or less exclusively with each other and have little realistic understanding of what is going on elsewhere in the society. Meanwhile, at the opposite end of the spectrum, those of low intelligence are left in an increasingly homogenous lower class, and the least intelligent are now congregating in a burgeoning underclass which is associated with the rise of many linked social problems (a large part of the book is devoted to demonstrating that it is low intelligence more than low social position which tends to generate poverty, crime, unemployment, welfare dependency, illegitimacy and political passivity). In parts of the inner cities, this has already led effectively to a "fundamental breakdown in social organization"[7] which has prompted the high intelligence élite to flee from the state schools and the urban centres and to seek security in new gated communities.

The most likely outcome of all of this, according to the authors, is the strengthening of a 'custodial state' designed to maintain order through intensified intervention and surveillance while leaving the 'cognitive élite' free to go about its business. In short, meritocracy is producing social fragmentation and polarisation.

Both Young and Herrnstein and Murray are pointing in their different ways to a problem which Durkheim and the functionalist sociologists of the 1950s completely overlooked. Meritocracy might work for those who have 'merit', but it seems to offer little to those who do not. Why should those at the bottom, those who fail, accept the results of meritocratic selection as binding upon them? Why should they accept that their intellectual 'superiors' should become their economic, social and political superiors?

This question raises three related issues associated with the growth of meritocracy. First, how can a meritocracy secure legitimacy in the eyes of those who fail (the problem of legitimation)? Second, how can it meet the expectations of those who succeed (the problem of 'positional goods')? And third, how can it avoid the paradox that human dissatisfaction often increases as opportunities expand (the problem of 'relative deprivation')? As society becomes more genuinely open, more genuinely meritocratic, so these three issues are likely to become ever more acute.

The problem of *legitimation* turns on the question of effective socialisation. If social position is determined at birth (as in a caste system), it is possible to prepare each generation for its fate. No false hopes are raised, no possibility of improving one's situation can be entertained. If social position is determined by a long-running talent contest, however, each generation spends its formative years anticipating the possibility of success, and the problem then arises of how to placate the eventual losers. Given that a meritocracy must be an open system, there is always likely to be a problem in educating the eventual losers to accept their fate.

The point can be illustrated with reference to an influential paper which was published in the *American Sociological Review* in 1960, before the English grammar school system was all but abolished. The author, Ralph Turner, pinpointed the different ways in which the American and British education systems at that time sorted out children for eventual occupational placement.[8] He recognised that extensive social mobility could occur within both systems, but the way in which it occurred was very different. In the American 'contest' system, many individuals competed for a limited number of prizes, and the contest was deemed to have been fair only if everybody was kept in the race right up to the bitter end so that their chance of winning was never taken away from them before the final result was declared. In the British 'sponsorship' system, by contrast, those individuals deemed to have the appropriate qualities were selected early for success (by means of the 11+ examination) and both the successful and unsuccessful were then put through training and socialisation appropriate to their future positions.

We need not debate here the relative merits of the two systems.[9] What is important about Turner's paper is that he recognised the fundamental problem faced by a contest system, namely, how to 'cool out' the losers. He cited research showing that American High School students at that time generally had hugely unrealistic expectations of their future career opportunities whereas the equivalent pupils in the British system were much more realistic. In Britain, realism bit harshly at age 11. In the United States, realism dawned slowly, often as late as the college years. A contest ideology, in short, is likely to breed major disappointment and resentment.

British education today has evolved into an American-style contest system. Selective schooling has virtually disappeared, and higher education has been opened up as a mass system, increasingly like that in America. This means that we now delay selection until age 16, or possibly even until age 21 (there is evidence that many employers are now recruiting graduates only from a select range of universities, for example). The paradoxical result of all this is that, as we have tried to extend the field of opportunity, so we have probably ended up making eventual failure that much more difficult to bear.[10]

This brings us to the second issue, the problem of *positional goods*. Put simply, the problem here is that, the more people who are enabled to succeed, the less value attaches to success and the more severe are the penalties of failure. Higher education is a classic 'positional good'—the more people who have it, the less valuable it becomes as a means of entering top positions, but the greater is the penalty for those who fail to get access to it at all, for a higher qualification becomes the prerequisite for entry to all sorts of jobs which previously did not demand it.[11]

Applied specifically to the phenomenon of social mobility and occupational selection, this means that membership of the middle-class is likely to be less advantageous the bigger that class becomes. When everybody else is working-class, it is a huge bonus to achieve upward mobility into the middle-class, but when such movement becomes common, the advantages decline. The more the opportunities for social mobility open up, therefore, the less they seem to offer. In such a situation, it is easy to see how a more open and fluid society may become a less cohesive and contented one.

This in turn leads us to the third issue, the problem of *relative deprivation*. There is a long and fascinating history of sociological research which demonstrates that individual dissatisfaction has more to do with relative than with absolute deprivation, and that the most acute resentment is often felt in situations of widening opportunity. In his classic analysis of data on satisfaction with promotion prospects in the American military, for example, Robert Merton found that those units with the highest promotion rates recorded the lowest levels of satisfaction, and vice versa. He reasoned that this was because high rates of promotion encouraged those in the ranks to compare themselves with those who had been elevated, with the result that they felt aggrieved at being passed over. Low promotion rates, on the other hand, encouraged identification with others remaining in the same position as oneself, and therefore fostered greater contentment.[12]

The implications of this for social mobility in society as a whole are obvious. With limited rates of social mobility, nobody expects to move up, and everybody is fairly contented with their lot. With extensive social mobility, many people move up, and those who are left behind begin to compare their situation unfavourably with that of their more successful peers. It is in this sense that a move to greater meritocracy is likely to generate increased frustration and resentment in society.

It seems that the ideology of meritocracy can be almost self-defeating. The more opportunities are held open for people, the more difficult it is likely to become to get those who fail to accept the result as legitimate, the less likely it is that those who succeed will feel any great sense of benefit, and the more resentful people are likely to become when they fail to emulate the success of their neighbours. These problems do not necessarily threaten social breakdown and fragmentation, but they can generate widespread disillusionment among successes and failures alike.

If meritocracy turns out to be so problematic, what are the alternatives? Assuming that we do not wish to return to the pre-modern system of social placement based on birth and inherited privilege (and even if we did, it is difficult to see, realistically, how we could), there are two major contenders.

The first, egalitarianism, is favoured by most contemporary critics of meritocracy. It would mean rejecting individual ability and effort as legitimate means by which people may strive to improve their situation relative to others, and moving increasingly to a system where status hierarchies are flattened and rewards are distributed with reference to some principle of a common citizenship entitlement. The second, libertarianism, favours abandoning altogether any attempt to link the allocation of social rewards to some principle of 'just' or 'fair' allocation, and accepting as legitimate any outcome provided it has not arisen from the explicit application of physical force.

The *egalitarian* case against meritocracy is essentially that it is morally wrong to reward people on the basis of their talents (and, perhaps, also their effort). Where meritocracy requires only equality of opportunity as the criterion of 'social justice', egalitarianism requires equality of outcomes ('end-state' equality).

There are two variants to the egalitarian critique of meritocracy. The first is already familiar to us, for it holds that there are no innate differences of ability between people and that talent, like effort, is merely the product of a privileged environment. Rewarding ability is thus tantamount to rewarding the children of the more privileged classes, which means that meritocracy turns out to be just another way in which dominant classes try to justify their continuing hold on top positions in society.

As we saw in chapter 4, many sociologists have adopted this line of attack, and it is one which remains common within so-called 'progressive' circles to this day.[13] Egalitarians basically dislike the idea of selection and competition and they would prefer a situation where there are no losers. They particularly dislike meritocratic selection because it seems to justify inequalities which they would prefer did not exist. As Daniel Bell has shown, this has led them to attack the very idea that there are any natural differences of ability between people, for to undermine the concept of intelligence is to undermine the very basis of meritocratic selection. If there are no natural differences between people, and if differences of ability arise simply out of unearned privilege, then it follows that nobody merits anything more than anybody else. In this way, the ideal of equality of opportunity is replaced by the much more radical ideal of equalising outcomes.[14]

This kind of argument is clearly vulnerable to the growing weight of evidence that there *are* natural differences between people, and this has given rise to the second variant of the egalitarian critique of meritocracy. This grudgingly accepts that there may be some innate differences between people, but denies that this is any reason to reward them differently. This is a much more interesting and challenging version of the argument, for it poses the pertinent question of why individuals should expect to be rewarded for talents which they were lucky enough to be born with and which they have themselves done nothing to deserve.

This is the position adopted by A.H. Halsey, John Goldthorpe's principal collaborator on the Nuffield College social mobility project, for he explicitly denies that what he calls the "liberal principle of 'justice as desert'" should be accepted as the criterion of social fairness.[15] The argument has recently been reiterated by Gordon Marshall and Adam Swift in a critique of my work on social mobility. Even if it were the case, they say, that ability alone determined class destinations, why should we equate ability with individual 'merit'? As they put it:

> It [is] particularly apt to ask whether an inherited characteristic—genetically-determined intelligence—is an appropriate basis for reward at all. A crucial issue here would seem to be the distinction between those attributes for which the individual can claim responsibility and those which are his or hers merely by chance. If someone possesses particular talents or skills merely as a result of the natural lottery then it is not clear how justice is served by rewarding such possession.[16]

Implicit in this argument is an appeal to a conception of social justice associated with the work of John Rawls.[17] Rawls suggested that we should gauge social justice with reference to the social arrangements which individuals would agree upon were they all in an 'original position' in which none of them knew what their personal attributes would be and all were ignorant of the place which they would occupy in society. Operating behind such a 'veil of ignorance', Rawls argued persuasively that we would all agree that resources should be shared out equally, except in those situations where an unequal distribution could be shown to produce greater benefits for those who are least well-off than they could possibly enjoy under any other social arrangement (what he called the 'difference principle').

Rawlsian logic suggests that meritocracy is inconsistent with social justice. In the original position, we would not choose to be born into a meritocracy because none of us could be sure whether we would be born bright or dull, and none of us would know whether we would be hard working or lazy by character. Furthermore, meritocracy violates the difference principle (e.g. by offering more training to the brighter people). The safest option for those in the original position would be to reject meritocracy and go for end-state equality—i.e. the egalitarian ideal.

The fundamental problem with this line of reasoning is, however, that the original position does not exist! In reality, we *do* know what abilities we have to offer, and we *do* know whether we are inclined to shirk or work hard (indeed, we can also do something to change these things by our own efforts). We know our potential and our inclination to use it, because these things are central to our characters—to what it is that makes us each a distinctive human being. To ignore them, as Rawls seeks to do in setting up his original position, is to treat us merely as clones of one another and to deny to us any responsibility for what happens in our lives.

Rawls's argument is profoundly anti-individualist and anti-humanistic. Denying us our our own personalities in the original position, Rawls happily arrives at the conclusion that the particular attributes of individual persons should be treated as the common property of the entire society. He does not go so far as to suggest eradicating all natural differences, but this is only because he wants to harness people's talents to the treadmill of the common good. He insists that, because talented individuals do not deserve their talent, it must be seen as a collective resource which must be devoted, not to the pursuit of individual gain or pleasure, but to furthering the interests of those who are least well-off.

Robert Nozick has developed a thorough-going critique of this whole approach.[18] He accepts that, viewed from the original position, social inequalities deriving from differences of natural ability would never be viewed as just, but he asks why we should approach the question in this way in the first place. In setting up the question of social justice as one to be resolved by people in the original position, Rawls has rigged the game. Only one result is possible—an agreement on end state equality—because all the information relevant to making a sensible judgement is denied to us. But why deny us this information?

In the real world, success is not some sort of natural resource which we find lying around waiting to be shared out. Success is achieved by individuals (often talented and hard working individuals) who, in the process, establish an entitlement to its rewards. Nozick gives the example of students taking an examination. Put into a Rawlsian original position and asked how the grades should be distributed, they would have little option but to agree on an equal share out. In reality, however, they would never agree to such an arrangement, for some of them have revised hard with the aim of getting good grades while others have spent every night in the bar. An equal share-out of grades would be seen by many of them as grossly unjust, and those who favoured it would more likely be motivated by envy or avarice than by any genuine desire to see justice done.

There is, in other words, an entitlement to reward which Rawls's approach deliberately suppresses. Why should those who have created their own rewards be expected to give them up to those who have made no effort? What kind of principle of justice is it that seeks to make the talented and the hard working the slaves of the least well-off members of their community without even asking why it is that the least well-off have so little as compared with them?

Nozick's critique of Rawls rescues the principle of meritocracy from the egalitarian critique. Following Nozick, the answer to the question posed by Marshall and Swift—why should we treat talent as deserving of reward?—is simply that the talented and hard working members of a meritocracy deserve their rewards if they have established an entitlement to them through their own efforts. If (as in the parable of the three talents), people with ability do not use it, then they establish no entitlement. It is not ability *per se* which is rewarded in a meritocracy; it is ability put to good effect. We do not select bright people into good jobs and pay them well simply as a reward for being bright. We do it (or, rather, employers and consumers of goods and services do it) because bright people *use* their ability in such a way that they generate resources, and this gives them an entitlement to the rewards which they earn from others.[19]

Even Karl Marx seemed to understand the logic of this. In his *Critique of the Gotha Programme* Marx famously defined the principle of communism as, 'From each according to his ability, to each according to his need' (an early formulation of the Rawlsian view that talent should be viewed as a collective good). But (unlike Rawls) Marx recognised that such a system could only work in a society which had overcome scarcity—a society where resources *are* 'lying around' in bountiful supply waiting to be allocated. This is why he placed communism at a point far off in the mists of future time, and devoted his more serious attention to the question of socialist distribution. Here, the principle was very different: 'From each according to his ability, to each according to his *work*'. Marx recognised that work performed by different people has a different value—one hour of labour by a talented and educated individual was worth more (and would therefore be rewarded more highly) than one hour of labour by an unskilled worker, the reason being that it creates more extra value:

> The right of the producers is proportional to the labour they supply; the equality consists in the fact that measurement is made with an equal standard, labour. But one man is superior to another physically or mentally and so supplies more labour in the same time ... This equal right ... tacitly recognises unequal individual endowment and thus productive capacity as natural privileges. It is, therefore, a right of inequality.[20]

Marx's principle of socialist distribution was essentially a meritocratic principle. But if meritocracy turns out to be consistent (theoretically) with socialism, does this mean that it is inconsistent (theoretically) with capitalism? The answer to this depends upon how we view the legitimacy of rewarding those who may not work hard and are not particularly talented, but who simply happen to possess property.

We saw earlier that Durkheim believed that inheritance was incompatible with genuine meritocracy. Clearly, Marx too envisaged a society where individual effort and ability would be fully rewarded but where capital would attract no rewards. The problem with these arguments, however, is that they point to a conception of 'meritocracy' in which people are allowed to reap the rewards of their own talents and efforts but are not allowed to decide how to spend them. Marx's argument, for example, is difficult to sustain in the context of a late twentieth century society where the majority of workers now indirectly invest a portion of their legitimate earnings in endowments and pension funds in order to accumulate property rights which are used to pay for their house purchases or to make provision for their old age. It surely makes little sense to suggest that individuals will be permitted to spend their incomes on immediate consumption, but will not be permitted to set some of this money aside in the form of savings and investments which accrue interest. How can it be legitimate for workers to spend their wages in the pub but not to spend them on a pension plan?

The important principle which arises here is that, if individuals are entitled to the money they earn, it must follow that they are also entitled to spend it as they see fit (provided only that this does not entail coercion of other people). This applies just as much to Durkheim's desire to abolish bequests as to Marx's desire to abolish investments. Where is the ethical basis for a principle of justice which would allow workers to spend money on their children while they are alive, but would deny them the right to transfer their money to their children once they die?

It is this line of reasoning which leads us to a *libertarian* conception of fairness based in a theory of just entitlement. Robert Nozick has outlined such an approach with great clarity. He argues that rewards follow entitlement and that entitlement can be established through three principles—just acquisition (established by producing resources oneself or through the freely contracted help of others), just transfer (through voluntary gifts or exchange), and rectification of past injustices (i.e. reallocation of resources in those cases where either of the first two principles has been violated). Put into practice, this means that individuals have a right to the money they have earned and to the money which others have freely given them.

Nozick's theory seems to pose a problem for the meritocracy ideal, however, for it is a theory of entitlement, not a theory of just deserts. It has nothing to say about rewarding talent or effort as such. It will often be the case, of course, that talented and hard working people end up establishing entitlement to substantial rewards, but this is in a sense incidental. Lazy people with little ability might also end up rich or successful—they might simply happen to find themselves in the right place at the right time, or they might inherit a company from their parents, or they might scoop the jackpot on the National Lottery. Luck, caprice, fluke, effort, all are equally legitimate as a basis for reward provided they involve no direct coercion of other people. The question of whether people deserve their good fortune is, for Nozick, irrelevant.

A similar argument is found in the work of Friedrich Hayek. With disarming frankness, he accepts that market capitalism can sometimes reward those whom we tend to think of as undeserving while meting out harsh treatment to those who display genuine merit. The talented individual who works hard but fails to find a market for his or her services will fail, just as the rogue who manages to convince others that they want what he or she is offering will succeed. For Hayek, there is nothing 'wrong' with this, and nothing to do be done about it. He assures us that in a free society, it will normally be the case that rewards flow to those individuals who put their talents to good use in providing a genuine service of value to other people, but he resists the idea that such an outcome should be engineered or enforced simply because we think of it as desirable:

> However able a man may be in a particular field, the value of his services is necessarily low in a free society unless he also possesses the capacity of making his ability known to those who can derive the greatest benefit from it. Though it may offend our sense of justice to find that of two men who by equal effort have acquired the same specialized skill and knowledge, one may be a success and the other a failure, we must recognize that in a free society it is the use of particular

opportunities that determines usefulness ... In a free society we are remunerated not for our skill but for using it rightly.[21]

This is a hard-nosed position which makes no compromises. Hayek is, of course, critical of the egalitarian position, arguing that the inherent differences between individuals mean that end-state equality could only be achieved by treating them unequally (i.e. unfairly). But, in the end, he is just as critical of the meritocratic position, arguing (like Marshall and Swift) that there is no credit to be claimed for talents which one happens to have acquired by accident of genetics, and that a meritocratic society would undermine liberty by fixing rewards according to people's attributes rather than according to their entitlements. For Hayek, as for Nozick, all that matters is that we should come by our success without coercing others, not that we should 'deserve' it.

It seems that having saved the meritocratic ideal from the egalitarian critique, we have ended up losing it again through a retreat into libertarianism. Neither egalitarians nor libertarians have any reason to be particularly interested in the kind of analysis of social mobility developed in this book, for neither sees any good reason why we should be concerned about rewarding talent and hard work. For egalitarians, what matters is that people should get the same at the end of the day, so if I end up in a low-paid, low status job because I have no aptitude for anything better, and you end up in a well-paid high status job because you work every hour of the day and pursue your ambition to its limits, the results are deemed unjust because they are unequal. For libertarians, what matters is that people should be able to keep whatever they happen to have freely acquired, so if I have no talent but am given a good job because my brother is on the Board, and if you are bright and committed but are denied an appointment because my brother happens to dislike the look of your face, no injustice has been done. Starting from opposite extremes, these two critiques of meritocracy meet, absurdly, in the middle.

Against both of these positions, the underlying premise of this book has been that it *does* matter why people end up in the positions they do. Both the egalitarian and libertarian positions have some intuitive sense to them, but in the end, they both founder on the fact that, in a modern society like contemporary Britain, there is a strong and shared sense of fairness and justice which demands that there be some link between individual talent and effort on the one hand, and reward through occupational success on the other.

Consistently with the egalitarian position, most of us do feel some sympathy for those who fail, but we also generally demand to know whether this has followed from their own stupidity or recklessness or was a result of circumstances largely beyond their control. This is precisely why the social welfare system for so many centuries attempted to distinguish the 'deserving' poor from the 'undeserving' and to treat them differently, and it is why so many people today feel angry at the thought that their hard work and personal effort is being taxed in order to support those who will not work as well as those who cannot.[22] Popular support for egalitarianism is always qualified by the question of just desert.

The same is true of support for libertarianism. Consistently with the libertarian position, few of us feel genuinely aggrieved by those who make good simply because they are 'lucky'. National Lottery jackpot winners are not widely resented for their good fortune, and although we may feel some envy when we hear of somebody who has come into an inheritance or has stumbled upon a new invention which makes them a millionaire, most of us simply shrug, smile, and mutter 'Good luck to them!'. We do, however, resent those who get to positions of wealth and influence through nepotism or the mobilisation of privileged social networks rather than through open competition, and we get justifiably angry about the allocation of positions on the basis of ascribed rather than achieved characteristics (e.g. allocation of jobs by race or gender rather than by talent or effort is widely held to be offensive).

Why are we generally happy to help out people who fall on hard times but not those who are feckless? Why are we happy to let lucky people enjoy their good fortune but not those who have gained success by virtue of their family connections? The common factor in all of this is a sense of fairness which holds that we should all be treated according to the same criteria. If I have to work in order to gain a living, then others who are also capable of working should not expect to live off my earnings. If I have to compete on the basis of my talent and effort in order to get a good job, then others should not be able to walk into top positions simply because they play golf with the boss's son. The lottery winner does not offend us because the rules are clear and we can all buy a ticket, and the beneficiary of a will does not offend us because we can all transfer money to anybody we wish. It is when the rules are bent such as to favour one party over another that the collective sense of justice gets badly bruised.

Nozick and Hayek try to reassure us that success normally coincides with merit (because, in a free market, rational buyers, including employers of labour, will choose the best services or products irrespective of the race, gender or social connections of those supplying them), but they accept that there is no necessary connection between the two, and they see no reason for government to step in to try to prevent 'irrational' discrimination against those with merit. Yet, as Nozick himself recognises, "People will not long accept a distribution they believe is *unjust*. People want their society to be and to look just".[23] This means that rules have to be established which ensure, as far as possible, that the competition which we are all entering is a fair one. It is simply not good enough to say that employers and others who are dispensing rewards have a right to use their resources as they see fit and can therefore decide on their own rules, for this will be seen as fundamentally unjust, and the cohesion of the society will suffer as a result.

There is, in the end, something unsatisfactory about a libertarian ethic which allows the 'deserving' to be disadvantaged without even trying to do anything about it, just as there is something unsatisfactory about an egalitarian ethic which allows the 'undeserving' to be advantaged without even trying to prevent it. Libertarians *do* have a problem in justifying caprice or bigotry as the basis for rewarding one individual while denying another, just as egalitarians *do* have a problem in justifying laziness or stupidity as legitimate grounds for doling out resources which other people have earned. Because both positions refuse to be drawn on the issue of merit, neither finally satisfies that generalised sense of fair competition on which the legitimacy of modern capitalist societies ultimately depends.

A few years ago, I organised a survey in which a sample of the British population was asked to respond to three different statements about the 'fairest' way to establish individual entitlement to material resources.[24] One of these statements represented the egalitarian ideal that "people's incomes should be made more equal by taxing higher earners." Just over half of the sample agreed with this while around one-third disagreed. A second statement expressed the free market, libertarian position that "people's incomes should depend on market demand for their services." Again, something more than a half of respondents agreed and around one-third disagreed. The final statement reflected the meritocratic ideal that "people's incomes should depend on hard work and ability". Fully 90 per cent of respondents agreed with this with fewer than 10 per cent disagreeing. Few moral principles can command universal assent in a modern, pluralistic, individualistic society, but meritocracy clearly comes pretty close.

This strong support for meritocracy relative to the other two positions reflects the fact that most of us understand that inequality is not necessarily 'unfair'—it depends on whether it is justifiable with reference to individual talent and individual effort. If we are convinced that, by and large, those who have the ability and who make an effort can usually find success, and that those who do not will not generally prosper, then the basis is laid for a society which should be able to function reasonably harmoniously. Meritocracy does have a problem in dealing with the social consequences of failure, but this need not be catastrophic as regards social cohesion provided the competition is known to have been fair. Ninety per cent agreement is not a bad basis on which to build and sustain a moral social order.

This is why the research findings outlined in this book are so important, for they give the lie to those who have consistently sought to undermine the legitimacy of the social order by convincing us that occupational recruitment is grossly unfair. I suspect that many of the social pathologies which have escalated so worryingly over the last thirty years in Britain—the spiralling rate of criminality, the growing denial of personal responsibility, the mindless pursuit of hedonism, the readiness to accept dependency—have something to do with the spread of an egalitarian ideology which has led so many of us to believe that social selection is rigged and that the dice are loaded. If people are increasingly led to believe that the competition is fixed, then of course they will conclude that it makes no sense for them to join the game. State dependency and criminality are then the only other games they can join.

But we have seen that occupational selection, by and large, is not rigged. The dice are not heavily loaded. The competition is not fixed. The game is worth playing, even for those born into the poorest social conditions. The sooner this message is learned, the sooner will the young and the disaffected come to realise that my father's teacher had a point all those years ago. The mountain-tops are within reach. All that is needed is the ability and the will to start climbing.

Chapter 1

1   Young, M., *The Rise of the Meritocracy*, London: Thames and Hudson, 1958, p. 94.

2   Jowell, R. and Witherspoon, S., *British Social Attitudes: The 1985 Report*, Aldershot: Gower, 1985.

3   Jowell, R., Witherspoon, S. and Brook, L., *British Social Attitudes: The 1987 Report*, Aldershot: Gower, 1987.

4   Bauer, P., *Equality, the Third World and Economic Delusion*, London: Weidenfeld & Nicolson, 1981, chapter 2.

Chapter 2

1   Heath, A., *Social Mobility*, London: Fontana, 1981.

2   'Britain's Richest 500', *The Sunday Times*, 14 April, 1996. Just 177 of the richest 500 individuals had inherited their wealth. Half of them had made their money from industry, commerce or retailing. Interestingly, the most common occupational background (other than the aristocracy) was coal mining—six of the richest 500 are the sons of miners.

3   Quoted in Goldthorpe, J., *Social Mobility and Class Structure in Modern Britain*, (2nd edition), Oxford: Clarendon Press, 1987, p. 21.

4   Bottomore, T., *Classes in Modern Society.*, London: George Allen & Unwin, 1965, pp. 16, 38, 40.

5   Miliband, R., *The State in Capitalist Society*, London: Weidenfeld & Nicolson, 1969, pp. 41-42.

6   Worsley, P., *Introducing Sociology*, Harmondsworth: Penguin, 1970, pp. 298, 301.

7   Giddens, A., *The Class Structure of the Advanced Societies*, London: Hutchinson, 1973, pp. 181-82.

8   Westergaard, J. and Resler, H., *Class in a Capitalist Society*, London: Heinemann, 1975, pp. 299, 302, 312.

9   Glass, D., *Social Mobility in Britain*, London: Routledge & Kegan Paul, 1954.

10   Payne, G., *Mobility and Change in Modern Society*, Basingstoke: MacMillan, 1987.

11   *Ibid.*, p. 89.

12   Marshall, G., Newby, H., Rose, D. and Vogler, C., *Social Class in Modern Britain*, London, Hutchinson, 1988.

13   Payne, G., *op. cit.*

14   Erikson, R. and Goldthorpe, J., *The Constant Flux: A Study of Class Mobility in Industrial Societies*, Oxford: Clarendon Press, 1992.

15   Scase, R., *Class,* Buckingham: Open University Press, 1992, p.53.

Chapter 3

1   Goldthorpe, 1987, *op. cit.*, pp. 327, 328.

2   Marshall *et al.*, 1988, *op. cit.*, p. 138.

3   For example, if 20 per cent of those from working-class backgrounds achieve middle-class positions, and 60 per cent of those from middle-class backgrounds achieve middle-class positions, there is a 3:1 disparity ratio in the relative chances of occupational success enjoyed by middle-class as compared with working-class children.

4   For an introduction to loglinear modelling techniques, see Gilbert, N., *Analyzing Tabular Data,* London: UCL Press, 1993. Loglinear models are useful in analysing data which are organised into discrete categories (such as 'social classes') as opposed to data which are measured on a continuous scale of equal intervals (such as income distribution or occupational prestige rankings). Although Goldthorpe's social class schema might look like a continuous scale, running from class I (the top of the service class) to class VII (the bottom of the working-class), he insists that this is not, in fact, a continuous hierarchy with equal intervals between each class position. Rather, he suggests that the only unambiguous hierarchy is that between the service class (classes I and II) and the rest, and that there is no necessary gradient between classes III and VII. This then rules out use of more traditional statistical modelling techniques, such as least squares multiple regression, and necessitates the use of techniques such as loglinear and logistic models which are designed for use on categorical data.

5   See, for example, Goldthorpe, 1987, *op. cit.*, p. 328.

6   Payne, 1987, *op. cit.*, p. 119.

7   As we shall see in chapter 9, this is an approach which owes much to the political and moral philosophy of John Rawls.

8   Goldthorpe, *op. cit.*, p. 114.

Chapter 4

1   In fact, they celebrated such differences. As Daniel Bell suggests, "There was equality, but in a Puritan sense of an equality of the elect. Among the Constitutional Fathers, the idea of virtue, and election by ability (if no longer by grace), dominated their thinking ... The central theme was independence, and the conditions whereby a man could be independent. But in the very use of Lockean language there was an implicit commitment to hierarchy—the hierarchy of intellect." (Bell, D., *The Coming of Post-Industrial Society*, London: Heinemann, 1974, p. 424.)

2   Gordon Marshall complains that this criticism ignores the fact that his work has tried to take differences of education into account (see Marshall, G. and Swift, A., 'Merit and Mobility: A reply to Peter Saunders', *Sociology*, vol. 30, 1996, forthcoming). As we shall see in chapter 7, however, educational qualifications on their own are a poor measure of ability, and they fail altogether to pick up on those bright individuals who achieve occupational success through routes other than credentialism. Furthermore, there is in this work no measure of motivation independent of achieved qualifications and occupational status (a weakness which Marshall recognises).

3   Dore, R., *Incurable Unemployment: A progressive disease of modern societies?*, London School of Economics, Centre for Economic Performance, Occasional Paper no. 6, 1994, pp. 2-3.

4   See, for example, Jackson, B. and Marsden, D., *Education and the Working- Class*, London: Routledge & Kegan Paul, 1962; Douglas, J., *The Home and the School*, London: MacGibbon & Kee, 1964; Bernstein, B., 'Education Cannot Compensate for Society', *New Society*, 26 February 1970, pp. 344-47.

5   Eysenck, H. versus Kamin, L., *Intelligence: The Battle for the Mind*, London: Pan, 1981.

6   Halsey, A., Heath, A. and Ridge, J., *Origins and Destinations: Family, Class and Education in Modern Britain*, Oxford: Clarendon Press, 1980, p. 208.

7   *Ibid*, p. 209.

8   Heath, *op. cit.*, p. 165.

9   For a review from both sides of the debate, see Eysenck versus Kamin, *op. cit.* Eysenck's contribution includes evidence on the internal and external reliability of IQ tests, and evidence drawn from work on reaction times and evoked potentials. See also Herrnstein, R. and Murray, C., *The Bell Curve*, New York: Free Press, 1994, for a discussion of recent experiments based on forward and backward digit span tests and reaction time tests, pp. 282-86; and Eysenck, H., 'Clever Measures', *Times Higher Education Supplement*, 27 January 1995, for a discussion of positron emission topography.

10   See Herrnstein and Murray, *op. cit.*

11   Mackintosh, N., 'Insight into Intelligence', *Nature,* vol. 377, 19 October 1995, p. 582.

12   Eysenck guesses that 50 genes could eventually be found to be shaping intelligence; Herrnstein thinks it could be 100. See also Lucy Hodge's interview with Robert Plomin, *Times Higher Education Supplement*, 22 December 1995.

13   *Ibid.*

14   See Palmer, A., 'All Men Are Not Created Equal', *The Spectator*, 17 July 1993, pp. 9-12.

15   Eysenck versus Kamin, *op. cit.*; Eysenck, H., *The Inequality of Man*, London, Temple Smith, 1973; Fulker, D. and Eysenck, H., *The Struc-*

ture and Measurement of Intelligence, New York: Springer-Verlag, 1979.

16   In Eysenck versus Kamin, *op. cit.* Similar figures are reported in Herrnstein, R., *IQ in the Meritocracy*, Boston: Little, Brown & Co, 1973, who also lists correlation coefficients for different types of blood relatives. Correlations are expressed by a coefficient, r, which varies between 0 (no correlation) and 1 (perfect correlation). By squaring a correlation coefficient, it is possible to calculate the proportion of variance in a dependent variable which is accounted for by the independent variable. For example, if variable X is thought to influence variable Y, and we find a correlation of 0.5 between them, we can say that X explains $(0.5 \times 0.5) = 0.25$ of the variance in Y.

Chapter 5

1   Goldthorpe, *op. cit.*, p. 328.

2   Bourdieu, P., 'The School as a Conservative Force' in Eggleston, J. (ed.), *Contemporary Research in the Sociology of Education*, London: Methuen, 1974, p. 32.

3   *Ibid.*, p. 42.

4   Bowles, S. and Gintis, H., 'IQ in the United States Class Structure' in Gartner, A., Greer, C. and Riessman, F. (eds.), *The New Assault on Equality: IQ and Social Stratification*, New York: Harper Row, 1974, p. 33.

5   See Eysenck, H., *Rebel With a Cause*, London: W.H.Allen, 1990; Herrnstein, *op. cit.*

6   Purvin, G., 'Introduction to Herrnstein 101' in Gartner *et al.*, (eds.), *op. cit.*

7   See *Times Higher Education Supplement*, 19 April 1996.

8   See, for example, Kamin, L., 'Behind the Curve', *Scientific American*, February 1995, who concludes that the book is "just a genteel way of calling somebody a nigger ... The book has nothing to do with science", p. 86. See also Palmer, A., 'Does White Mean Right?', *The Spectator*, 18 February 1995, pp. 9-11; and the various contributions to Fraser, S. (ed.), *The Bell Curve Wars*, New York: Basic Books, 1995; and Jacoby, R. and Glauberman, N. (eds.), *The Bell Curve Debate*, New York: Times Books, 1995.

9   For evidence on average IQ scores of children born to fathers and mothers with various different levels of IQ, see Preston, S. and Campbell, C., 'Differential Fertility and the Distribution of Traits: The Case of IQ', *American Journal of Sociology*, vol. 98, 1993, pp. 997-1019, table 2.

10   Marshall, G. and Swift, A., 'Social Class and Social Justice', *British Journal of Sociology*, vol. 44, 1993, pp. 206 and 197 respectively.

Chapter 6

1   A 'normal' distribution is one where most people score at or around the average for the whole population, and there is a 'tailing off' in the number of people scoring above or below this point. Height is an obvious example of a normal distribution, for many people are within a few centimetres of the mean height of the whole population, and there are progressively fewer people at each height as we move further away on each side from this mid-point. Many features of human populations turn out to be approximately normally distributed. It is likely, for example, that parental affection is normally distributed—most parents would score around the average if it were possible to measure such a phenomenon accurately, and progressively fewer would be found as we moved towards the extremes of complete indifference and total, smothering, love. The same is probably true of motivation (only a few people are extremely lazy or extremely hard-working, while most fall somewhere between the two), of housing conditions (few of us live in either slums or mansions), of quality of teaching (most of us most of the time are probably taught by averagely-good teachers), of ability (which is why IQ tests are constructed in order to produce a normal distribution of scores with a mean of 100), and of many of the other factors which have often been identified as important in influencing children's chances of occupational success. We shall see later that our initial assumption of a normal distribution of ability is fully justified by Goldthorpe's findings, and that the assumption need not therefore depend on any prior knowledge of the normal distribution of IQ in reality.

2   In a variable that is normally distributed, the mean, the mode and the median all fall at the same point. In the case of IQ, the mean score of 100 is also therefore the modal score (i.e. more people score 100 than any other single score).

3   Eysenck versus Kamin, *op. cit.*

4   Cited in Eysenck, *The structure and Measurement of Intelligence, op. cit.*

5   Halsey, A., 'Genetics, Social Structure and Intelligence', *British Journal of Sociology*, vol. 9, 1958, pp. 15-28.

6   Eysenck versus Kamin, *op. cit.*, p. 64.

7   Herrnstein, *op. cit.*, chapter 4.

8   *The Intelligence of Man, op. cit.*, p. 139. I am indebted to Dr. Rod Bond for his work in calculating this coefficient from the data cited by Eysenck.

9   Pawson, R., 'Half-truths About Bias', *Sociology*, vol. 24, 1990, p. 239. My original critique was published as 'Left-write in Sociology', *Network*, vol. 43, 1989, pp. 4-5. For criticisms, see Marshall, G. and Rose, D., 'Reply to Saunders', *Network*, vol. 44, 1989, Payne, G., 'Competing Views of Contemporary Social Mobility and Social Divisions', in Burrows, R. and Marsh, C., (eds.), *Consumption and Class*, Basingstoke: Macmillan, 1992; Crompton, R., *Class and Stratification*, Cambridge: Polity Press, 1993.

Chapter 7

1   Looking first at class of origin, the social class of fathers of panel members was last collected in 1974 (sweep 3) when the children were aged 16 and when 14,761 of them remained in the panel. The percentage of these fathers occupying each class position can be compared with the class distribution of all males at the 1971 census (although it has to be remembered that most of the fathers will have been in middle age at this time while the census reflects the occupations of all males including those much younger, who may still be on an upwards trajectory):

	Panel Fathers (1974)	All Males (1971 census)	% over/under represented
R-G class:			
I	5.4	4.7	+15
II	20.0	17.1	+17
IIIN	9.6	11.3	-15
IIIM	44.4	37.0	+20
IV	14.8	17.2	-14
V	5.8	8.2	-29

As regards the social class achieved by panel members themselves by age 33, comparison can be made (for males) with the social class distribution of men at the 1991 census (again remembering that we should not expect the occupations of a cohort of 33 year-olds to match those of the whole male population between 16 and 65):

	Panel Males (1991)	Census Males (1991)	%over/under represented
R-G class:			
I	7.4	4.7	+15
II	32.3	17.1	+17
IIN	10.7	11.3	-15
IIIM	33.3	37.0	+20
IV	12.9	17.2	-14
V	3.4	8.2	-29

Both tables indicate that the most significant bias created by panel wastage has occurred as a result of the under-representation of those born into and/or entering class V (unskilled manual work).

2   In the original NCDS data, low scores on the motivation scale indicate high motivation. Because this is counter-intuitive, and hence potentially confusing, the scale has been reversed here.

3   See Goldthorpe and Hope (1974). This scale is used because it provides a dependent variable measured at interval level. This enables multivariate analysis based on least squares regression and (in chapter 8) the development of a path model derived from structural equation models. Goldthorpe himself abandoned this scale (in favour of a categorical class schema) when he applied log-linear modelling

techniques to the analysis of social mobility tables, but regression-based models remain more appropriate if the concern is to understand how different individuals end up in different positions, as opposed to Goldthorpe's major concern with analysing the effects of relative mobility rates on class structuration. For a discussion of these issues, see the papers by Kelley and Marshall, together with Goldthorpe's reply, in Clark, J. Modgil, C. and Modgil, S. (eds.), *John H. Goldthorpe: Consensus and Controversy*, London: Falmer Press,1990.

4   The fact that ability has a clear effect over and above its association with educational qualifications is further evidence that we cannot rely (as Marshall does) on paper qualifications as substitute indicators for IQ when attempting to explain patterns of social mobility - see footnote 32.

5   Variables entered/deleted stepwise with p<0.05 as criterion for entry and p>0.10 as criterion for deletion. Missing data replaced by group means based on gender.

Chapter 8

1   The model presented here was developed mainly by my colleague, Dr. Rod Bond, with whom I am now working on the NCDS data. I am most grateful to Dr. Bond for the huge amount of work which he put in to producing this model, and for his permission to reproduce it here.

2   There are various measures of the degree to which a model like this fits the data. All are expressed on a scale from zero to 1, and convention dictates that the degree of fit should exceed 0.90. In the model outlined in figure 5, the Goodness of Fit index equals 0.975—a very high degree of fit for a model of this complexity.

3   It should be noted that, as we move through the path diagram, the coefficients relating to later variables express only their additional effect, not necessarily their total effect . Ability at 16, for example, has a loading of only 0.11 on qualifications achieved at 16, but we see that ability at 11 also loads directly on qualifications at 16 with a Beta of 0.34. The coefficient of 0.11 gives us the *additional* effect of ability at 16, after the effect of ability at 11 has been taken fully into account.

4   On the motivation scale high scores equal low motivation, which is why the correlation coefficient is negative.

5   The correlation coefficient is negative because father's class is scaled from a value of 1 = middle-class to 3 = lower working-class. Therefore, the 'higher' the class the lower the score on this variable.

Chapter 9

1   See MacFarlane, A., *The Origins of English Individualism*, Oxford: Blackwell, 1978; and Abercrombie, N., Hill, S. and Turner, B., *Sovereign Individuals of Capitalism*, London: Allen & Unwin, 1986.

2   Durkheim, E., *The Division of Labour in Society*, London: Macmillan, 1933 (first published in France, 1893).

3   Anthony Giddens has recently made a similar point in his critique of fundamentalism—see Giddens, A., *Beyond Left and Right*, Cambridge: Polity Press, 1994.

4   *Ibid.*, pp. 375-77.

5   I have reviewed this theory in more detail in Saunders, P., *Social Class and Stratification*, London: Routledge, 1990.

6   *Op. cit.*

7   Herrnstein and Murray, *op. cit.*, p. 522.

8   Turner, R., 'Sponsored and contest mobility and the school system', *American Sociological Review*, vol. 25, 1960.

9   I cannot, however, restrain myself from noting that in Germany, which we think of as being so much more successful economically and so much more cohesive socially than either Britain or America, they continue to select children early rather than delaying it.

10   One of the ironies in all this is that a principal argument which used to be put against educational selection at eleven was that it was socially divisive and emotionally fraught for those who failed to achieve a place in the grammar schools. The move to comprehensive secondary education has almost certainly made this problem worse, however, for the dull are (in theory at least) now kept within sight and reach of the brightest throughout their school careers, only to fall to the wayside at sixteen. In reality, of course, many of them jump before they are pushed, which may help explain why there is such a huge problem of truancy, disruption and disaffection in the British comprehensive school system today. Similarly in higher education, the disillusionment and cynicism of the students who make up 'Generation X' may well result from the dawning recognition that despite clutching a lower-second degree from a new university, the glittering prizes are still out of reach. Problems of legitimation and social cohesion are likely to be much greater in a society which gives one-third of its young people degrees and then offers them jobs as shop assistants than in one in which degrees are limited in the first place.

11   A positional good is one whose utility declines the more other people gain access to it. See Hirsch, F., *Social Limits to Growth*, Cambridge MA: Harvard University Press, 1976.

12   Merton, R., 'Contributions to the Theory of Reference Group Behavior', in his *Social Theory and Social Structure*, New York: Free Press, 1957. See also Runciman, W., *Relative Deprivation and Social Justice*, London: Routledge & Kegan Paul, 1966.

13   A good example is Polly Toynbee's attack on my research findings in *The Independent on Sunday*, 17 December 1995. For Toynbee, the very idea that social mobility might be a product of innate intelligence is 'lethally dangerous', and work like mine is dismissed as ideology masked by a 'veneer of science'. For her, it is self-evident (as 'any pushy parent knows') that intelligence can be dramatically changed by paren-

tal intervention (in fact, as we saw in chapter 8, parental ambition for children has virtually no impact on their IQ level).

14   Bell, D., *op. cit.*

15   Halsey, Heath and Ridge, *op. cit.*, p. 6.

16   Marshall, G. and Swift, A., 'Merit and Mobility', *op. cit.*, publication is forthcoming; reference is to typescript page 19.

17   Rawls, J., *A Theory of Justice*, Oxford: Oxford University Press, 1972.

18   Nozick, R., *Anarchy, State and Utopia*, Oxford: Basil Blackwell, 1974.

19   Nozick points out a contradiction in Rawls's own argument which is relevant to this. The difference principle allows for inequalities where they benefit the worst off. This implies that the most talented and hard working may need to be paid more to encourage them to produce resources from which the least advantaged can derive benefit. It follows from this that talent can legitimately be rewarded, but this flies in the face of Rawls's insistence that talent is a pooled common resource which does not entitle those with talent to claim the rewards which flow from its application.

20   Marx, K., 'Marginal Notes to the Programme of the German Workers' Party', in Marx, K. and Engels, F., *Selected Works in One Volume*, London: Lawrence & Wishart, 1968, p. 320.

21   Hayek, F., *The Constitution of Liberty*, London: Routledge & Kegan Paul, 1960, p. 82.

22   For a good recent discussion of this issue, see Green, D., *Community Without Politics*, London: Institute of Economic Affairs, 1996, chapter 5.

23   Nozick, *op. cit.*, p.158.

24   Saunders, P. and Harris, C., *Privatization and Popular Capitalism*, Buckingham: Open University Press, 1995.